FOURTH LEADERS

Printed in Great Britain

FOURTH LEADERS

FROM

THE TIMES

1956

A selection

from the past

twelve months

LONDON

THE TIMES PUBLISHING COMPANY LIMITED

PRINTING HOUSE SQUARE

CONTENTS

	PAGE
DIRECTIONS FOR USE	1
BASIC BEANIE	3
THE TEMPTATIONS OF TIDINESS	5
ON NOT BEING TIED DOWN	7
THE LUSCIOUS COOLING ICE	9
THAT RINGS A BELL	11
JAUNTY JOHN	13
THE BRITISH PRAM	15
ON THE WING	17
THE BROWSER	19
WALLPAPER	21
SINS OF SOCIETY	23
ALL YOU WANT EVERYWHERE	25
THE RETURN HALF	27
ALL WOUND UP	29
LET THE JUDGES SING	31
READING AT MEALS	33
THE CAPTAIN HOGS THE SCREEN	35
UNDER THE PLATE	37

	PAGE
GRAND SLAM	39
CLUBS AND THE LIMELIGHT	41
GOING OVER HOUSES	43
FOCUS ON FREEDOMS	45
IN THE MEDICINE CUPBOARD	47
ON PROBATION	49
WELL	51
VANISHING LORE	53
GONE AWAY	55
SEAMY SIDE UP	57
PARISH PERENNIAL	59
LOCAL AUTHOR	61
DOMESTICATED DUMBO	63
VOLES PREFER COX'S	65
THE ODD HALFPENNY	67
A PAIR OF BLUE STOCKINGS	69
TWO TUNES ON A DRILL	71
HERE, LET ME TRY!	73
A WALLET FOR OBLIVION	75
DAILY DOZE	77
WORMS TO THE RESCUE?	79
THE NEW FLAG	82
THE BABIES' LEAGUE	84

	PAGE
THE TOWN HALL	86
MYSTERY MEN	88
BUT SOFT! FURNISHING	90
U-HEALTH	92
BUS IN URBE	94
NO HARD FEELINGS	96
MISS GREEK GODDESS, 1956	98
THE DRESSING GOWN	100
ALIAS PUSSY	102
ORWELL THAT ENDS WELL?	104
BANJO ON MY KNEE	106
ABSENTEES ALL	108
BOILING DOWN SCOTT	110
THE BOTTOM DRAWER	112
IN HOT WATER	114
LOOKING FOR GRANDFATHER	116
TYPISTS ON THEIR TOES	118
FIVE POUND FOOLISH	120
SAY IT WITH IAMBICS	122
SPRING IN THE PARK	124
HOLIDAYS FOR HORSES	126
GHOSTS IN THE CELLAR	128
B FOR MUTTON	130

	PAGE
WIGGLES TO THE RESCUE	132
FLAG DRILL	134
MICE ON THE MARCH	136
MIND MY EGGS	138
THE ONLY HOPE	140
A POVERTY OF POETS	142
ANY OLD PIERS ?	144
DEVON DUMPLINGS	146
TWENTY THOUSAND LEAGUES UNDER	148
GIFT FISHES	150
PUTTING OFF TILL TO-MORROW	152
OUT OF DOORS	154
THE MASCOT PLAYS THE GOAT	156
NOT WIMBLEDON	158
STEALING THE FLOWER SHOW	160
THE GHOST GOES EAST	162
TAMING THE BENS	164
WOMAN DRIVER	166
TIME FOR BREAKFAST	168
ESCAPE ME EVER	170
APPEALING	172
ASSIGNMENT TO CLEETHORPES	174

DIRECTIONS FOR USE

THE parent is on the brink of an exacting time during which many qualities, such as stamina and tolerance, will be called into play. He may avoid the more ludicrous and violent ordeals—impersonating Father Christmas, being the central figure in Blind Man's Buff, or the victim of a practical joke—but if Christmas goes anything like according to tradition he will not escape the role of chief demonstrator. There are among the presents some rudimentary forms of amusement that get under way without parental guidance, but sooner or later a child's voice, slightly overwrought, will detach itself from the general hubbub and ask : " What are you supposed to do with this ? "

The demonstrator's time has come. He must drop whatever he is doing and see the matter through to the end. In this field his wits are not likely to be as sharp as the child's and he is therefore obliged to consult the inside of the lid. The directions have several splendid virtues. They are brief, simple, and to the point ; the only trouble is that so often he is totally unable to carry them out. He may be an authority on nuclear fission, he may have a thorough grasp of the working of the World Bank and still be at a loss to interpret simple written instructions involving the use of the hands. This sensational new game, he reads, will keep the kiddies amused by the hour. You have only to follow the directions and that, to judge by the enraptured, rubicund faces in the picture on the lid, is easy enough. The inference is obvious : any fool can do it, and yet . . . " Hold the loose ends of the string between forefinger and thumb and draw them slowly towards operating end, reversing the process until the

1

side sections are raised to the required level. . . ." This sort of thing is all very well, but in practice it can be so utterly bewildering as to make the operator believe he must be holding the sensation upside down or that half of it is missing.

Even at meals he is not safe. Just when his digestive organs are needing all the help they can get, one of those curiosities out of a cracker is rescued from the floor and placed before him. " Cut along the lines as indicated. Draw the strips of paper together and nip in between fingers. . . ." As the parent goes fumbling on, scratching his chin and re-reading the blunt phrases, he becomes increasingly conscious under the stare of critical eyes that he, not the toy, is being judged. The same discomfiture attends him as he tries to interpret the rules of a game " for four or more players" or to decide how to attach a key piece of mechanism to some futuristic engine of war. At long last the inert machinery springs to life, the last piece falls into place, the rule resolves itself, every thing is ready for the lighted cigarette. Once again the directions have creaked through to success, but delay has been fatal. Attention has, more often than not, been diverted elsewhere, and the demonstrator enjoys his victory alone, reflecting that what is simplest is not always the most easily understood.

BASIC BEANIE

A NEW YORK store is, it appears, trying to make the English school cap popular among American boys, and, as a somewhat dubious first step towards this laudable end, has labelled it a " basic beanie with a narrow visor." Presumably the store has been content to leave it at that and has not gone into the complex questions of status that divide school caps from one another and invest certain of them with an awesome importance and prestige. " Collins," remarked the hero of *The Loom of Youth,* " see that cap hanging over the ' Sir Galahad ' picture ? Yes, that's it, the Second Fifteen cap. Do you mind just flinging it on the top of the cupboard over there ? Thank you. The thing is not worth having now." This unconventional treatment of a cherished possession was occasioned by the football captain's injudicious act in giving second XV caps to a side which had defeated a scratch team of Essex Yeomanry brought up on soccer and lacrosse—the time was 1914—by a score which approached three figures. The hero felt that the glory of the cap was being cheapened, and his bitterness emphasizes the gulf that divides the cap awarded for outstanding performances on the field of play from the cap—the basic beanie in fact—that every member of the school, down to the humblest new boy, is entitled to wear. The latter can be snatched from the heads of unsuspecting companions and sent whistling down the wind, stuffed carelessly into the pocket, or rolled up and used for drop-kicking practice ; the former is almost too precious to wear.

It is not, however, only school caps that need a boost ; the whole tribe of caps could do with one. The fashion

3

for Edwardian clothes has not extended to that article once to be found in all well-stocked wardrobes, the travelling cap. But then, although the cap on occasions ventures into higher realms of society, it is, in essence, proletarian—" cloth capped " is the approved adjective for the multitudes, especially in the North, that attend professional football matches. Again, an age deeply suspicious of anything it can lump under the general head of snobbishness may see in it a symbol of the customs of a vanished and decadent age. It was the cap, not topper nor bowler, nor even homburg, that was traditionally held in hand—although all three may well find themselves falling into the part played by the cap during interviews with present day, tigerish bank managers. But the odds against this cap, as against all other forms of head-gear, staging a notable come-back are considerable. Too many people prefer nowadays to go bare-headed, and the most popular form of basic beanie, if the phrase will bear the interpretation, is the hair.

THE TEMPTATIONS OF TIDINESS

MOST untidy people have vague and unfulfilled aspirations after tidiness and are always meaning to turn over a new leaf. At the present moment they are bursting with jealous admiration of Grundisburgh, which has just won a trophy as the tidiest village in all Suffolk. Last year it was beaten by Chatsworth by a bare three points, represented, for all we know, by a single cigarette carton deliberately planted in the road by a sinister stranger from a rival village. This year it trimmed and brushed and clipped away harder than ever and has metaphorically hit Chatsworth for six. Tidiness is undeniably a very pleasant thing and never more so than by contrast. "Everything clean and comfortable," said Mr. Weller as he enumerated the charms of the inn at Towcester on that pouring wet night, and then, carried away by the spirit of alliteration, "French beans, taturs, tarts and tidiness." So the picture of Grundisburgh in its neatness is peculiarly enviable as we look at our own room, with reference books skirmishing on the floor, with ink pots dangerously poised, and writing materials hopelessly imprisoned under a mass of old newspapers. Almost it persuades us to make an heroic start in reducing things to some kind of order, but it is a delicate task requiring the dexterity of a spillikins champion. A single book is coming out beautifully inch by inch when one unlucky touch sends the whole cascade in motion and no clutching hand can arrest it.

At such a moment our mood changes and we suddenly realize that we hate tidiness. Is there not something priggish about it ? Better a hundred times to hunt daily through that cag-mag of rubbish than seek after a

5

Grundisburian perfection which is wholly beyond us. Admittedly there have been some very great men who were also very tidy men. DICKENS was one of them; he could not work unless certain specified objects were set out in their right places on his writing table. In consequence, no doubt, he created one or two deplorably tidy heroines. They jingled bunches of keys in baskets. Esther Summerson spent two hours before breakfast counting little drawers and cupboards, making notes about jam on a slate, and being " generally a methodical old-maidish sort of foolish little person." Should we like to marry Esther Summerson or even to resemble her ? And the same question applies to Agnes Wickfield, another basket jingler. If we answer the question honestly it is clear that we never intended to be tidy. We must be content with envying Grundisburgh the luxury of its own feelings.

ON NOT BEING TIED DOWN

TENNYSON gave short shrift to the romantic young lady who believed that the birds in the high hall garden could have been anything except rooks. But he behaved in a much more human—if not in a much less gruff—manner when the BISHOP of RIPON asked him whether the people were right who asserted that the three Queens in the barge which came to collect King Arthur were Faith, Hope, and Charity. " They are right and they are not right," said TENNYSON. " They mean that and they do not. They are three of the noblest of women. They are also the three Graces . . . I hate to be tied down." We cannot but sympathize with TENNYSON at this time of year. We return from our holiday. " Did you have a good time ? " asks Jones. " Yes," we reply, full of remembered pleasure. " Where did you go ? " " What did you do ? " " Did you visit A ? " "And see B ? " "And call on D ? " Suddenly conscious where we have not been, we become vague, and evasive, and miserable. It is even worse when the same kind of thing happens before we go away.

To be described as vague is, in this business-like, mathematical age, in a way to be criticized. And yet how much happier we are when the world still has some blurred edges left. That is how we start out in childhood, and shades of the prison house of facts and definitions and punctuality and preciseness close around us all too fast. Are there any better years than those when the clock face is still only a picture, and a watch a thing that makes a noise ? Then each morning's morrow is so far away as to be beyond possible measure. Sad is the day when we get

7

knowledge of our first time-table. Some part of us has died when it includes that of the celestial omnibus.

TOLSTOY is perhaps the greatest tier-down there is in literature. He never leaves you in any doubt as to precisely how his characters looked, what they were, or what he intended to happen to them. Yet we have never seen an edition of *Anna Karenina* or of *War and Peace* that did not lose something by being illustrated. In one sense, indeed, it can be held that, so far as *La Gioconda* is concerned, PATER was a greater artist than LEONARDO and that both outdid Nature. The attraction so many of our modern artists exert may well be that you can make anything you like of their paintings. The same squiggles on the same highly coloured background can be entitled " Nausicaa at the Launderette " or " Mercury astride a Space Satellite " and give us equal pleasure. So let us go on treating the formula for nuclear fission as nothing more than a pretty design ; not knowing whether Pip married Estella ; shutting our ears to any record that purports to be the actual song the sirens sang ; and refusing to read authentic discoveries about the later life of Isopel Berners. Science may some day shatter our world, but at least scholarship can leave us our dreams. Mortal will be our enmity towards the man who ever digs up the indisputable portrait of HELEN.

THE LUSCIOUS COOLING ICE

THESE are days in which the mind turns naturally towards ice-cream. Not as a food—for though we are told it is that, who wants food when it is so excessively hot ? Not as a medicament—though it is asserted that there are (or were some years ago) hospitals in America where the patients are fed on nothing but ice-cream. But merely as one of the most agreeable of refreshments, a very pleasant means of cooling off. This, of course, is a thing of which too great advantage can be taken. Many a small boy has brought misfortune upon himself, and upon those in charge of him, by too free an indulgence. Yet the classical instance of too much ice is that of the grown-up hero of the celebrated early Victorian comic song of *Shivery-Shaky*. He, it may be remembered, was tempted with a " luscious cooling ice " by a pastry-cook when " The day was hot enough to kill, And he kept tasting them until It gave his corpus such a chill, He never again got warm." What melancholy events ensued ! He gave chills to all his friends ; his wife left him ; and finally " In a hot bath he was found, The water frozen all around The man who couldn't get warm."

The grim warning of that song, as sung to early youth by a beloved grandfather, though it may have ensured a measure of restraint, has never killed a liking for a good ice-cream. Sadly one must admit that ices, like so many other things, are not what they were. The best of all were those made at home (in a little churn surrounded with broken ice and salt) of real fruit juice and cream that came, in those far days, from cows. Sometimes, alas ! the making was not quite a success, and what emerged from the churn (if the maker wearied too soon

9

of turning its handle) was cool and semi-liquid, rather than cold and firm. There was indeed a terrible occasion when the salt got into it. But when success did come—what a triumph it was ! And could anyone ever decide whether raspberry, or black currant, or strawberry gave an ice its most delicious flavour ?

To-day the ice-cream for dinner comes from a shop, which gets it from a factory, and no one but a scientist would venture to say what it is made of, except that it is something very chemical and hygienic. Yet, for all that, there are advantages. The old exquisite flavour of the home-made ice is perhaps seldom met with to-day. But then the modern ice is more plentiful than the old—and very nearly ubiquitous. It is, moreover, though generally limited to two or three varieties, nevertheless quite pleasant to the taste. Hateful as the admission is, there is something to be said for mass-production. Even elderly and respectable persons welcome the moment when, in their stalls at the theatre, there is brought to them the choice of " Tub or choc-ice ? " And only the most snobbish of them would be shy of admitting that, for just a moment (until perhaps the thought comes back of poor Shivery-Shaky), what they would really like to answer is " Both."

THAT RINGS A BELL

HIGH Business Executives are asked to consider many things these days. There is still one thing, however, which it can be doubted whether they have considered at all. That is the bell. There are bells and bells. It is not enough merely to classify them in such loose categories as church, shops', door, office, and hand. Within the world of the ordinary office alone, there exists, somewhere or other, pretty well every possible kind of bell ; and how well the secretary who has moved around a bit knows most of them. There are the " angry bluebottle," the " drowsy mosquito," the " cup-tie rattle," and the " dying duck," with every possible variation in between. The bell-pusher—pardon, the High Business Executive— in the next room knows nothing of the murderous thoughts their discordance arouses. It says much for the will-power—we will not believe it is deceitfulness—of the trim young things that they generally manage to come into the presence smiling. There was once an H.B.E., more sensitive than most—or perhaps it was that he just liked gadgets—who had things fitted up so that, when he wished to summon her, his secretary's bell played a little tune. But such is the frailty of both human nature and things man-made that after the novelty had worn off she began to think the whole idea silly ; then, later still, the last note of the little tune ceased to function. This made her so mad, always waiting for the tune to finish, which it never did, that she took another job where the boss just shouted for her.

Bells are not what they were. Is there any more moving experience than to go into the kitchen of some quite modest, middle-class house, and see the pathetic sight

11

of the derelict bell board. There they are, all the little windows, with their " First Bedroom," " Second Bedroom," " Dining Room " and so on, silently reminding us of another age when the red or striped indicators behind them would go on quivering after the clatter had died down so that the folk in the kitchen would know where we were summoning them from. Now, most of the time, we are in the kitchen ourselves. And when, by some mischance, once in a blue moon, the bell does ring, how startled we are. We look up, see the " Drawing Room " is agitated, hastily take a census of ourselves to see we are all there, and feel like the heroine in *The Cat and the Canary* or some Methuselah-like gold prospector suddenly invaded after sixty years living alone in an abandoned ghost-town. Then " It must be the window cleaner " someone declares, and we all breathe a sigh of relief, while Willie goes off to tell him he has left his step-ladder leaning against the bell-push. Maybe the old inhabitants of the kitchen would have remained if we had made the bells, and other things, more attractive. Maybe the day will come when the outside offices will similarly be deserted, and H.B.E., having dictated his letters to himself, will be found typing and stamping them. It is a disastrous thought—but no more revolutionary than what has happened in the home. Perhaps we should rip the old buzzer out and try the effect of a set of Westminster chimes.

JAUNTY JOHN

IF diplomatic courtesies are exchanged in the next world, there must be some delicate drafting going on there at the moment. A rare, posthumous compliment has been paid to a statesman who died ninety years ago. A street in the capital of the Republic of Dominica has just been named, at the request of its PRESIDENT, after LORD PALMERSTON. What will all those distinguished shades, whose lives on this earth he so ruffled, think about it ? From TALLEYRAND and METTERNICH to LINCOLN and BISMARCK, the chanceries of Europe and of the New World felt the sting of his irrepressible pen and tongue. He was an ardent follower of TALLEYRAND'S definition of non-intervention—" mot métaphysique et politique qui signifie à peu près la même chose qu'intervention." This delighted small nations and the little man in the street at home—and none the less because BISMARCK was dismissed as " the crazy Minister at Berlin " and other great heads, some of them crowned, received hearty thwacks.

" Mamma England's spoilt child," he was called by the fastidious, who lamented that, the more outrageous his behaviour became, the more admiringly the old lady cried, " What a spirit he has !—smash goes the crockery !" But he was also a past master at narrowly avoiding a smash. He was never downhearted. When the Cabinet was wondering what to do about GARIBALDI, he cheerfully remarked, " Do ! Oh, let's marry him to the rich Miss ——," and swept away the objection that he already had a wife with " We'll get GLADSTONE to explain her away." He had a long innings. At sixty-five he was judged by LORD JOHN RUSSELL to be " too old to do much in the future." Within two days of his eighty-first birthday,

13

when he was Prime Minister, he breakfasted off mutton chops and a half glass of old port, regretted that he had " lived so long without discovering what a good breakfast it is," and peacefully died.

No wonder that so many at home and abroad delighted in Pam or " Cupid "

> With his hat o'er his eyes and his nose in the air
> So jaunty, and genial and debonair
> Talk *at* him—*to* him—*against* him—none
> Can take a rise out of Palmerston.

Certainly the shades will not now be able to do so—not even that of the QUEEN, who found him " Really too bad and most disrespectful." They will be bound to congratulate him ; for when last did one of his contemporaries in any high office have a street named after him ? But there is one shade who will sincerely be delighted. His EM will think it no more than right. When he had turned eighty and they were staying at Brocket, with two young couples in the house, he drew EM's arm into his and said, " Here we are, three pairs of lovers."

THE BRITISH PRAM

IT was good to read, in an account of the purchases made by visitors to our shores, that the British perambulator is held in high esteem among such shoppers for its superior finish and proud carriage. It is held in high esteem by many natives of these islands too, though they do not propose ever to buy another and though " finished " rather than " finish " would be the appropriate word to apply to the last perambulator they had anything to do with. It was battered and wheezy and squeaky when, its duty done, they persuaded the reluctant dustbin men to take it away, and there was more of relief than regret in their hearts as they watched its passing. Yet regret was there, too, mixed with their memories of the many miles they had propelled it, of struggles to get it on the back of modern taxis ill-equipped to take such things, of getting it in and out of guards' vans, with or without a sleeping occupant. They remembered, perhaps, the mingled pride and embarrassment with which they made a *début* with it and its contents, and the different sort of embarrassment, entirely free from pride, which they felt when impelled in busy streets to insert a screeching infant in the conveyance against its will.

These are parents' memories, but there are childhood's too. There are some who can reminisce quite glibly about what they felt when they looked out on the world from a baby carriage, and many more who, though incapable of this feat of recollection, are perfectly informed of what they did and said and looked like, so often have they gazed upon a pop-eyed reflection of themselves in the family album and listened to the fond tales of their

15

fathers and mothers. They reflect a little wistfully sometimes upon those days when, in MAX's phrase, " I had,
and wasn't, a perambulator." They achieved at that early
age a peak from which all else has been decline. Never
again—with all respect to the air line advertisements
and the announcements of the shipping companies—will
they travel in such luxurious ease, with minds so free from
care and attendants so alert to satisfy their every whim.
Though they grew in time heartily sick of their transport,
they remained at the same time rather attached to it.
Just as, when they evolved into parents themselves, they
came to feel both warm and cold towards their children's
—British—pram.

ON THE WING

WHATEVER else changes in the view out of an aeroplane window, the wing is always there. Sometimes, it must be admitted, the long grey slab can be a nuisance, getting in the way of a splendid sight of the Queen Mary in mid-Atlantic or of a sunset on the hills of Oman or of one's own diminished backyard. But there it is, and everyone who has flown for long hours ends by becoming quite attached to the wing. He is equally sure, such are its qualities, that it will remain attached to him. He has not the slightest doubt about it, having looked upon it and mused upon it in fair weather and foul. It takes on its own distinct character, the character of an elder brother. It is steady, unassuming, dependable, uncomplicated. The test pilot in the American cartoon who yelled through the wireless : " Say, are these wings *supposed* to flap " was not only badly frightened ; he was as incredulous and outraged as a man whose faithful dog, the companion of many years, had bitten him. A wing simply does not flap. It does not do anything much. It may shudder a bit in a storm, taking the strain, shaking the rain from itself. It is unmoved when sparks and sheets of flame (apparently unnoticed by the pilot) spurt so disconcertingly out of the engine. It lets bits of the engine glow, red hot, upon it. Things, like wheels and flaps, come out of it and go back again. It remains unmoved, like the Guards on parade.

A proper tribute to its sound qualities has been too long delayed " The company regrets to announce that Flight Number so-and-so is delayed a couple of hours." It may be something to do with the pressurizing, or the pumping system, or the retractable undercarriage. But who ever

17

has heard that it is because the wing has gone wrong ? It would be like blaming a late dinner on a sudden fault in the dining table. The men who used to stroll upon it in mid-air, while the crowds below waved and applauded, knew that it would never let them down. In the age of gadgets it remains simple, solid, and serene. The traveller has only one niggling little complaint to make. Often, in black night, one wishes it had a larger light on its tip, the better to be seen by other flying machines. Perhaps that is merely part of its essential modesty, but why not give it a larger light as a belated tribute ?

THE BROWSER

" TIRED of play, Rupert made his way listlessly into the library." That is how it might have started in a novel of fifty years ago. It ended some time later when Rupert, having pulled down and rejected a number of rather valuable, if dull, volumes in half calf, was found by his distracted mamma absorbed in GOLDSMITH'S *Animated Nature,* or perhaps a lighter work which she was surprised to find that her husband possessed. Rupert, though he may not have realized it at the time, had become a browser. Not all random readers came to the pleasure in such solid comfort as Rupert. Some may have had the luck to make the acquaintance of *Brigadier Gerard* and FOXE'S *Martyrs* curled up in an armchair before the fire, but probably more started their random reading with *Pears,* or some battered edition of the *Children's Encyclopaedia,* propped up behind a piano on which someone was practising scales.

But, whenever or wherever it was, what started as an innocent pleasure, and is indeed the magical open gateway to all the unending joys and profits of really reading books, can also become something of an anti-social habit. The irredeemable browser dispatched by his wife to the library for a light romance returns empty-handed and late for tea having got no farther than the Travel and Adventure bay where WHYMPER'S *Scrambles in the Alps* caught his eye (and who shall be surprised at this ?). Yet he suffers himself for his pastime ; his business man's three-course luncheon is apt to be reduced to a cup of coffee and a sandwich because there is a new biography in the bookseller's near his office and he is reading it in instalments. Deprived of his regular pastures, he can improvise with success. He will contentedly occupy himself with outdated works of reference while waiting for an appointment and, during a sermon not notable for originality of thought, he will be more likely to plunge into a reappraisal of the Thirty-Nine Articles than to doze off. He can, in fact, improve the shining hour almost anywhere on almost anything.

And that, perhaps, is his best defence against criticism. And criticism there is. For, too often, he is held in but low esteem by his fellows, who deem him a dabbler, the possessor of a grasshopper mind, and quote POPE'S familiar lines about the effects of learning to describe him. This, surely, does him less than justice, for on the one wet week with which his chosen resort has been afflicted in a splendid summer, the browser is found to be the least disconsolate member of his family. He is discovered engrossed in a treatise on poultry-keeping which he has found in a wardrobe. " By Jove," he says, as a drenching shower smudges the window panes, " this is interesting ; I never knew there was so much to keeping a few hens. Raining, is it ? Ah, well." One feels that even POPE would have had respect for such a one.

WALLPAPER

THE reluctant handyman—" Got to be handy these days, old man, whether you like it or not "—feels sometimes that he could write a book about wallpaper. It would provide an outlet not for erudition but for emotion. There would be little in it about Papillon or Réveillon or John Baptist Jackson of Battersea or WILLIAM MORRIS, but a great deal about awkward corners, and papers that " bubble," and the difficulty of doing ceilings, and the way in which builders never seem to succeed in building a room exactly on the square. One bit of history, perhaps, the author might put in—the fact that in early days people often nailed the paper to the wall. He has sometimes been tempted to do something like that. How easy it might be with drawing pins.

In spite of failures, in sequel to modest successes, he finds that the subject—indeed the art—begins to grow upon him. Few occupations can satisfy so swiftly and completely as papering a room can the human need to bring order out of mess, beauty out of little back bed-rooms. The man with the brush and the stepladder has the feeling of creating a not contemptible work of art. It should live at least for a year or two, and if covered up then by layers of later work may come to a kind of con-cealed immortality, unsuspected until future generations, digging about in the ruins, discover his wallpaper and wonder how he did it.

His wallpaper. He thinks of it as that, though he did not design it. He chose it, and that, he is persuaded, is quite as difficult. Difficult—but pleasurable and fasci-nating ; in many ways, in fact, the pleasantest part of the whole. This is the moment of vision, the ecstatic moment

21

which, as in other arts, goes before the labour of performance. The vision proves sometimes to have been a little
blurred or crooked, and the result, when got upon the
wall, to be more like a page from a children's comic than
a picture out of *Vogue*. But good or bad as the end may
be, he has had that happy beginning, whether in some
bright shop in the suburbs, or in a West End showroom
where they take your name at the door and invite you to
be seated on a sofa before a small sloping desk, and
place books of paper on the desk before you, and drape
pieces over a kind of easel, while an elegant young man
in a dark suit patters of colour schemes at 95s. a roll.
After an hour or two of that—and this is essentially a
matter in which time had better be no object—a man
goes out into the sunshine, or the rain for that matter,
looking on the world with different eyes, seeing even in
the ladies' frocks (he had not noticed it before) reflections
of the stuff he has just chosen for the attic, hints for
future panels for the parlour.

SINS OF SOCIETY

EVEN in the naughty nineties, which saw the report of the Parnell Commission and the trial of OSCAR WILDE, the Baccarat Case is unsurpassed as a *cause célèbre*. It drew from CHIEF JUSTICE LORD COLERIDGE probably the first known enunciation of the dictum " this Court is not a theatre." The memories that were stirred when the card-table from Tranby Croft was put up to auction in Hull are of the conflict of two civilizations and two moralities that contended for the soul of the Victorian age, and with that age are now indifferently buried. The proceedings in Court on the slander action, with the fashionable beauties on the bench, the sketch-books and opera glasses and rounds of applause, fell in fact between the two essential trials. In the first trial, in the privacy of Tranby Croft, the *haut monde* had passed sentence on one of its own number, a baronet and a Guardsman, for its own special deadly sin of cheating at cards After the jury in Queen's Bench had upheld that judgment—which nevertheless will always be disputed—the *bourgeoisie* tried the principal witness, no less a person than the PRINCE of WALES, for the sin of playing cards at all.

From the other side of Lethe the shade of the PRINCE REGENT must have been as bewildered as the millions of poolsters would be to-day to know what all the hubbub was about. But England was convulsed, and the monarchy shaken. This journal, in the name of " the serious public —who after all are the backbone of England," expressed at considerable length its profound regret " that the Prince should have been in any way mixed up, not only in this case, but in the social circumstances which prepared the way for it." The greatest Victorian of all was in no

23

doubt to which of the two moralities her sanction ought to be given. The then EDITOR of *The Times,* in his old age forty years later, used to tell of a note that came to him from a very august quarter, to the effect that the QUEEN had taken note of the leading article on The Conduct of the Prince of Wales, and entirely agreed with the EDITOR : that HER MAJESTY had sent for HIS ROYAL HIGHNESS (then in his fiftieth year) and had read him the article.

And still no one knows whether SIR WILLIAM GORDON-CUMMING did or did not alter his stake after he had had a glimpse of the cards. Except to his descendants it can no longer greatly matter, for the whole social order which was to be tested by his guilt or innocence has vanished away. Tranby Croft is now a girls' school ; and if there is whispering of illicit games of canasta in the dormitories, the scandal can be safely left to the prefects on the spot. It is no use darkening the room for a séance in which the green-baize table with the rounded ends can be made to tap and reveal the secret of sixty years ago. It is too little sophisticated. It was never a real baccarat table at all : only a makeshift that somebody dug out and put in the billiard room for the second evening's play, after the three ill-matched whist tables which were put together on the first night had been found too uneven for the croupier's rake.

ALL YOU WANT EVERYWHERE

Bookshops, unlike others, are not very much affected by seasonal change, and their windows are not perceptibly different as the months pass ; but soon there will be one difference at least and that is the replacement of the little piles of foreign phrase books. The appearance of these bright, rather boastful (all you want in France, Germany, Italy) little publications marked, like the swallow, the coming of summer, the start of holidays : their disappearance marks autumn as surely as the first mist. The phrase book, covering every contingency from shopping to the loss of limb and luggage in tornado or armed assault, was a deft invention. For about six months they have sold steadily and their purchasers, with indifferent skill, have made constant use of their invaluable, if somewhat peremptory, contents. For phrase books are remarkably sharp. The man, for instance, who in England might diffidently request his taxi driver to try to reach Victoria by nine, will find himself, when using a phrase book, saying abruptly : " Go faster, my man ; hurry ; pray drive more carefully—stop ! "

It is difficult to imagine how tourists ever managed without them. Presumably, while travel in past years was less general, and certainly far less casual, there were more people equipped for it than undertook it rather than the other way about. Theoretically, young ladies were capable of tackling France, though it is doubtful whether in fact their knowledge went far. Becky Sharp was engaged by Miss Pinkerton because of her ability to speak " French with purity and a Parisian accent " which was " in those days rather a rare accomplishment." MR. KENNETH ROBINSON, in his biography of WILKIE

25

COLLINS, tells us how, on the Grand Tour undertaken by DICKENS, WILKIE COLLINS, and AUGUSTUS EGG, WILKIE wrote to his mother saying that ". . . Egg was engaged in a desperate struggle with the Italian language and found it impossible to remember what he had learnt." Even BORROW, indefatigable in his desire to learn more and yet more languages, recognizes that the passion is not general when, wishing to have his revenge on Belle, he says : ". . . you shall have this evening the longest lesson in Armenian which I have yet inflicted upon you."

Whether BORROW would have approved the short-cut method of learning languages offered by the phrase-book is doubtful, but the unhappy EGG would surely have welcomed it. For to-day his problems would have been infinitely greater. He would, for instance, scarcely have had time to struggle with the Italian language if he had travelled by air. Now a traveller may well need to speak several languages within a few hours, a feat requiring an orderly as well as an informed mind. Perhaps, the remedy does, after all, lie in phrasebooks, streamlined to instruct the traveller, simultaneously, on the customs, dangers, advantages, foods, and illnesses of a dozen different countries in a dozen different tongues.

THE RETURN HALF

MOST people have now come home from their holidays, but there are still a few for whom the sands have not yet quite run out. To those few this consolation may be offered that they need not have the additional misery of hunting wildly for the return halves of their railway tickets. Save for such concessions as cheap days, excursions, or the like, return tickets have now become a hollow mockery. The time-tables continue to set out the fares—single so much, return so much ; but the holiday maker with the smallest arithmetical faculty has long since discovered that the return fare is exactly double the single down to the meanest penny. Here, to be sure, is no financial gain. Far from it, indeed, by comparison with older and happier days, but at least the born loser is no longer tried past endurance by the problem of how and where to keep the return half in security. There were always some travellers of an obviously dashing and capable exterior who would hand over the whole ticket to the collector with a noble gesture, allow him to tear off the right half, and then put it away carelessly in a pocket where it would be found perfectly safe at the holiday's end. Others, conscious of their own fallibility, would at the earliest moment secrete the odious, elusive little document in the innermost corner of a wallet and even so be tortured by recurrent doubts. A return half is second only to an old silver threepenny bit in a malign capacity for hiding itself.

It may be remembered that the famous French blue-beard, M. LANDRU, whenever he escorted one of his victims down to that secluded little country cottage of his, was said to take one single and one return ticket.

27

This may have been only a grim joke on a reporter's part, but M. LANDRU was a man of method and of an economical turn of mind. For those of us who are less systematic it is a real relief to the feelings to hand over the outward half and start afresh, even though, if the money gave out, the return half would at least ensure that we were not marooned. One ticket might not be too intolerable a burden, but the paterfamilias who had those of the entire party in his care was bowed down by his trust. Moreover, even if put away safely " in a fire-proof chest vith a patent Brahmin," the ticket is a constant reminder that holidays are the most fugitive of joys. It can be the rose-leaf that keeps the princess from her sleep. It would be interesting to know whether the ticket pocket is to-day a less common feature of coats than it used to be. The tailor, in measuring his customer and inquiring as to the number of pockets, used always to suggest one. Perhaps he no longer deems it necessary, now that to get there and back costs twice as much as to get there.

ALL WOUND UP

"IT winds itself up with the slightest movement of your hand," says the advertisement with cheerful confidence and undoubted truth. The trouble is that not until you have begun to wear your first automatic wrist watch do you realize, with dismay and a sinking feeling, how slight the movements of your hands are. Every other part of your body seems to be in a state of constant agitation. But your hand ? Good heavens, how long is it since you last moved your hand ? It seems to have been an unconscionable time a-lying. Inactive and inert, it cannot possibly have been doing its new job. There can be no doubt about it. The watch must be running down. It may stop any moment. Suddenly you become wrist conscious. You flick it this way and that. You stroke your hair (if any) or your head. You put your arm into a vigorous military swing as you pace the dozen steps across the room. Your secretary comes in unexpectedly and is astonished to find you apparently practising to be a tic-tac man. The pundits who used to tell you to put " plenty of wrist into it " as you drove off from the tee would be delighted to see you now. Then it seemed advice impossible of accomplishment. Now you find yourself putting your wrist into everything you do. Your wife notices with amusement how deliberately you now turn your teacup (and listen) as you drink. Your friends are puzzled at the fervour with which you pump their hands. Your enemies are prepared to swear you have been seen to shake the wine bottle. Hitherto an undemonstrative man, your talk acquires the accompaniment of a wealth of Italianate gestures.

29

After a time, of course, it begins to wear off. There are, indeed, moments when you are sure you have done with such nonsense. Admittedly, the first—and worst—phase is over. All the same, you cannot see what possible harm it can do to brush your teeth somewhat longer than you used to do. Rather, it should do good in more ways than one. (Commercial television might get on to this : " Wear an automatic wrist watch and you will never wear dentures " has possibilities as a slogan.) You can be found even to have a persisting urge to brush your boots. The experts may smile and say that all this is easily avoided. All you have to do is to get a watch which tells you how much " power " it has left. How little expert they are in human nature. The indicator seems to run down so much faster than it runs up. True, in some miraculous way it always does seem to get replenished, but it eases anxiety to keep helping it on. If you leave your watch off when you go to bed it seems to have lost an awful lot of " juice " by morning. If you keep it on— in order to avoid this—it has lost so little that you can come only to the conclusion that you must have had a restless and wretched night. And every time you look at the indicator you begin to do sums with time. Suddenly the day comes when you realize you have not done this for a month or more. You have not even thought of the watch running down—and there it is, still cheerfully going. Exactly at what moment it escaped your consciousness you will never be able to determine. Like dropping off to sleep, it happened because it could not be registered.

LET THE JUDGES SING

IT must have been frustrating alike for the litigant and for his counsel to be told, the other day, by a Viennese judge, after they had obliged with songs in court, that he was so unmusical that he had been barred from singing at school. Their object was to convince him that there had been plagiarism, and first the composer of one of the controversial ditties and then his lawyer sang their plaintive notes. But his Lordship refused to be a musical DANIEL come to judgment. Taking advantage of the judicial prerogative of blandly confessing ignorance, he seems to have based himself on what GILBERT said to SULLIVAN—only a rash man asks me to hum. A psychologist might detect in this a desire, suppressed and strong, to make the welkin of the court room ring. His Lordship may have something in common with a once famous Master of Balliol, DR. JENKYNS.

That endearing little scholar, around whom (and not excluding his white pony) so many legends clustered, is said, on the highest oral authority, to have sent for an undergraduate on a winter morning after chapel. " I hear, Mr. Rogers," the MASTER began, " that you sing." The charge was not denied, and it was pressed home. " I hear, Mr. Rogers, that you are a good singer." Witness confessed that his indulgent friends said that he was. " You sing a song called ' Jolly Nose,' Mr. Rogers ? " He admitted it. " Sing it now, Mr. Rogers." And sing it the vocalist did before escaping to his breakfast. History has never related why the MASTER commanded this performance. Is it possible that he, like the Austrian judge, had been made to take the wrong turning at school ?

Songs are too seldom heard in open court. The lyric forced from MR. ROGERS would hardly, it is true, help in any action.

Nose, nose, jolly red nose,
And who gave thee this jolly red nose ?

seems inapplicable to any conceivable plea likely to win over the bench. But " I know I'se to blame " from " Bill Bailey, won't you please come home ? " might soften one of their Lordships (and there are such) with long and distant memories of the music-halls. So might " Everybody's doing it now " in a parking case. " I can't tell why I love you, but I do " may savour of unconvincing sycophancy. A real genius in this line of pleading would strike up something in the chorus of which his Lordship had irresistibly to join. But what song is a judge most likely to sing ? It is a speculation as dark as is the old one about the sirens.

READING AT MEALS

SOME people feel lost without something to read in bed, and have even been known in their despair to fall back on the old newspapers lining the chest of drawers. Others utterly eschew reading in bed and presumably compose themselves with one long happy sigh as their heads touch the pillow. But even these severe and fortunate creatures have never declared the book at bedtime to be a positive crime. It is otherwise with reading at meals. This is deemed by some stern persons an unsocial and unsociable habit, a waste of the good food provided by Providence, a promoter of gobbling and indigestion. At breakfast they may possibly admit the toast and hot newspaper, but otherwise they regard it as thoroughly immoral. And yet even those in charge of us in our youth did not wholly abhor it. There are some who will still recall with pleasure a scene, now sadly distant, from teatime at their private school. At a certain eagerly expected moment there came a voice from the dais announcing that those who had finished might read. This was followed by a sound as of a clap of thunder, as everybody picked up a book from the floor and brought it down on the table with a cheerful bang. Instantly the tablecloth sparkled with red and green and gold bindings of the immortal works—it was a long time ago—of MR. G. A. HENTY. At the thought of that scene *The Lion of the North, The Dragon and the Raven,* and *The Young Carthaginian* come flooding back with a poignant freshness and the taste of thick and not very exciting bread and butter.

In much earlier days Tom Brown noticed at his first dinner at Rugby that the prepostor read all the time he was eating and it was a " hard-looking book " that he read. That no doubt would have pleased DR. ARNOLD, who detested a lack of seriousness among boys due to their reading such light-minded works as *Pickwick* and *Nicholas Nickleby*. To-day in grown-up life there are moments when we would gladly read even a hard-looking book at meals if manners would permit. A book is admittedly something of a reflection on a neighbour, even on a perfect stranger in a restaurant car. It can be a strong shield against the assaults of a pathetic loquacity. It does not envelop the reader as does a newspaper but has perhaps a more determined and repulsive air. It will hardly be received well at a club of which the tradition is that everybody talks to everybody else. Putting aside these defensive purposes a book can add a pleasant relish, and even a long drawn out lingering delight to a meal. He who is a solitary either by choice or necessity will find in it much comfort. What kind of a book he should read must be a matter of individual taste, but clearly he must not become so engrossed in it as to let his food grow cold. HENTY would not do nowadays, alas, but there is much to be said for a book in which each page is as the winding of a familiar lane with every tree an old friend. A good bed book makes a good meal book.

THE CAPTAIN HOGS THE SCREEN

THE news that H.M.S. Ark Royal has been fitted with television diffusion equipment " which can be used both for operational and entertainment purposes " merits closer and more serious appraisal than it has received at (for instance) the Cavalry Club. This is not a development which can be dismissed with tasteless jokes about " Kiss me, Harding." In the history of a great naval power few more significant innovations (or so it would seem to the layman) have taken place since the invention of the rowlock, which is now, of course, some considerable time ago. What beneficent changes will be wrought in the rough life of our brave sailor-lads ! The days are long past when a captain, if he wished to address his crew, had to assemble the scum (as he often affectionately called them) on the poop before bawling out his latest ultimatum. Most of HER MAJESTY's ships are now equipped with some form of public address system, whereby orders can be transmitted from the bridge to the more outlying portions of the vessel. Not only, however, is this a soulless and impersonal procedure, but it is apt, by reminding him too vividly of the train— the dear, homebound train—now standing at Platform 14, to increase the dejection of a young sailor already suffering from nostalgia.

The new system has everything to recommend it. The captain's personal signature tune will call the attention of all hands to the screens, softly refulgent in bulkhead and gun-turret ; and a moment later there will be the captain's great face, speaking to them. It will be instantly apparent from his manner whether the purpose of the transmission is operational or recreational ; the crew will quickly learn

35

to sense whether the parrot on his shoulder represents *panache* in the face of a critical situation or an accessory to the patter with which he customarily introduces a solo on the flute. They themselves will certainly be given a chance of exhibiting their talents to their mates in the new medium, and the captain may face, in time, a problem of some delicacy both from the artistic and the disciplinary point of view. If he too frequently fades out their favourite crooner in order to interpolate complex and unwelcome instructions about de-gaussing the after marlinspike (or whatever it may be) the audience-reaction will not be a healthy one. Too much of this sort of thing, and he will have to forget all the lessons he learnt from LADY BARNETT and SIR MORTIMER WHEELER, put back the clock and order all hands up to the poop.

At the War Office the Navy's latest departure has displaced the tonsorial tendencies of national service men as the problem of the hour. Though it is clearly desirable that a military commander in the field should have no less adequate facilities for impressing his personality on his subordinates than are provided for a naval commander at sea, nobody can quite see how this is to be arranged. The difficulties of (so to speak) tying an elaborate tin can on to a tail already due for docking seem insuperable. The Royal Air Force nurtures, or pretends to nurture, a faint hope of being able to instal television in some of its larger flying-machines. But it is only in the Secret Service, where the time-honoured tradition that nobody must know anybody else by sight still holds sway, that envy does not rear her ugly head and a self-righteous equanimity prevails.

UNDER THE PLATE

INTREPID is the dinner guest who, attracted by the design of the plate put before him will boldly turn it over to find out the maker's name. Rather will he resort to all manner of devices rapturously praising the chrysanthemums which form so handsome a background to his hostess and furtively taking a quick look while her self-satisfied back is turned ; or else he will drop his handkerchief, tip the plate up slightly, and try to perform the incredible feat of seeing the name on the upswing. There is something to be said for the poor guest. When in fact he does take his courage and the plate in both hands, his hostess as likely as not hastens to explain that it is neither Ming nor Sung (if they made plates) but was bought at the village stores. He does not know whether to say that this was obvious to him all along or to express incredulity. A dreadful diffidence pervades the whole conversation and soon the rest of the table are looking around to see what has happened, with the same kind of awareness that one has when the clock suddenly stops. The ideal thing would be, of course, for the guest to be able to turn the plate upside down, scrutinize it, make a note of the address in his pocket book if he so wishes, and for the hostess to pay no attention. But even this can have its hazards. If the plate is left too long reversed the hostess may think she has placed her guest wrongly according to Burke, Debrett, Kelly's Directory, or the Almanach de Gotha.

Considering the important part they play in our lives, lamentably little attention seems to have been paid by poets, folklorists, fairy-tale tellers, and others to plates. (The willow pattern is a lonely exception.) Few quotations

37

about plates come to mind. There is EDNA ST. VINCENT MILLAY'S

> That now, domestic as a plate,
> I should retire at half-past eight

which does not seem to make much sense. SHAKESPEARE appears to come to our aid with Cleopatra's magnificent panegyric on Antony

> in his livery
> Walk'd crowns and crownets, realms and islands were
> As plates dropp'd from his pocket.

but while we are wondering what the plates were doing in his pocket in the first place, our eye is caught by a learned footnote which tells us they were silver coins.

This neglect of plates is all the more remarkable when one considers the great attraction they have for children. After all, a great deal of a healthy child's pleasure comes off a plate. Equally, of course, there is the fact that pretty pictures are put at the bottom of children's plates in order to induce them to eat up quickly. Maybe it is the reaction from such duplicity which in later years shows itself as a general masculine indifference to plates. Or, more likely, it is because up to now—at least where the talking and writing has been concerned—this has been largely a man-made world. Now that sons and husbands, as well as wives and daughters, have to take a hand in the washing up, they may become a little more interested in plates.

GRAND SLAM

" SHUT the door ! " thunders the voice of authority
from behind the newspaper, and the precipitate
rush from one boyish activity to the next is reversed in
mid-passage. It is one of childhood's clearest memories
and close behind it comes another, the same voice, more
aggrieved, reproaching us now for having slammed the
door. Thus early in life we are made door-conscious.
Later we learn the subtle uses to which the handling of a
door may be put. BARRIE remarked that it was wonderful
how much you could conceal between the touch of the
handle and the opening of the door if your heart was in
it. No less wonderful is the amount of meaning that can
be read into the closing of a door. Connoisseurs of
human behaviour can distinguish between the bang of
indignation, the slam of finality, and the firm restrained
securing of the catch that indicates mounting vexation or
passive resistance.

Outside in the open air these niceties disappear, and a
regular orgy of slamming is indulged in. An observer at
the French motor show, struck by the silent closing of
doors as visitors climbed in and out to inspect the latest
models, deduced that here was a new development in
car design. On inquiring he was told that for years car
doors had been made to close silently and that the
motorist only slammed doors because he enjoyed it. It is
not quite fair to fasten all the blame on to him. There
may be in the flinging to of a car door a sense of emanci-
pation from the conventions of the home or the release
of some pent-up emotion, but there are other explanations
just as convincing. Some car doors, warped and racked
through the years, simply cannot be closed except by an

all-out assault upon the coachwork, but, these apart, there is a strong suspicion attaching to car doors on the part of the public.

The door of a room is either shut or not shut, but for some reason that is not altogether clear car doors have an intermediate position, one in which they are not properly shut. They go off, as it were, at half-cock, and the ensuing fuss—the nagging rattle, the warnings uttered, the slowing down of the vehicle, and the final heave that recovers the position—have been the bane of drivers for years. No doubt the latest models have well-behaved doors that respond to the slightest touch, but the superstition rooted in past experience that safety lies in violence lingers on. In time, no doubt, it will disappear, and its place may be taken by a realization that in the car-lined streets of towns the banging of car doors is nearly as unwelcome as the slamming of the study door at home. A quicker solution might be for the designers—who are men of ingenuity, for have they not contrived so many different ways of opening a car door that a stranger trying to get out is almost certain not to turn the right knob the right way ?—to go a step farther and make a car door that cannot be slammed.

CLUBS AND THE LIMELIGHT

"HE'LL be lunching his father at the Garrick soon." This filial act was to be made possible by the purchase of a portable typewriter. Thus equipped the young man in the advertisement wrote a successful novel, an achievement which (we were asked to infer) almost automatically ensured his election to the Garrick Club. It is customary for new members of any club to allow a considerable period to elapse before they summon up the courage to entertain a guest within its initially rather intimidating portals ; and during our (as it were) novitiate most of us would, for a number of scarcely definable reasons, be as unlikely to invite our father to the club as we would our bank-manager or our old house-master. This young man, thanks probably to the morale-building qualities of his portable typewriter, had no such foolish inhibitions. " Larry," we can hear him saying, " I should like to introduce you to my Pater." He will clearly go far.

Interesting though he is, he is less interesting than this new development in the relations between clubland and the advertising world. Although it pays to advertise, and few clubs enjoy an economic position of unassailable strength, it somehow never seems to have occurred to the committees of, for instance, White's or the Athenaeum that they might benefit, in the same way that seaside resorts, the armed services and the lesser-known girls' schools do, by a little judicious advertising. This dignified if somewhat clueless attitude has been respected by the advertising profession. Although a club often provides the *mise en scène* for an advertisement, it is seldom any particular club. It is certainly not our own, its members being more uniformly distinguished in appearance, its port glasses larger and its servants more deferential. It is a kind of dream-club, the Junior Nirvana, perhaps, or the National Elysium. Monocles are much worn in it, and though the leather armchairs are almost infinitely capacious nobody has ever been seen to sleep in them.

Surely, now that the ice has been broken, this tradition of anonymity can be discarded. Clubs need not go so far as to advertise themselves. But they could sponsor, or be sponsored by, firms to whose products their urbane and mellow atmosphere would lend a certain lustre.

" By Jove, Sir Terence, this tinned spinach simply melts in one's mouth ! "
" Naturally, old boy. It's a Poshfood Product. We generally manage to look after ourselves pretty decently at the Turf."

Apart—so far, at any rate—from ladies' underclothes there is almost no form of merchandise whose sales would not be stimulated by the sort of background which only a good club can provide.

" That's a devilish well-built pair of galoshes, Alaric. Who do you get to make them for you ? "
" Nobody, Sam. I always buy Squelch's Imperial Overshoes. Most of us do at the Travellers."

It will be interesting to see, when the time comes for the club bore to be portrayed as a victim of night-starvation (THINKS : " They seemed to be quite *interested*. I must be losing my grip "), which club he belongs to.

GOING OVER HOUSES

THE question which is the worst line of poetry ever written will always remain undecided. Every one of us had his favourite which he whispers lovingly to himself and will strongly uphold in argument. WORDSWORTH at his most prosaic was a mighty champion, but there are two lines of TENNYSON which demand consideration, since in addition to their superb flatness they have a fine journalese or house agent's touch,

> Let us see these handsome houses
> Where the wealthy nobles dwell.

The sentiment at least is admirable and statistics lately given show that it makes every year a wider appeal; the number of visitors to historic houses rises steadily. This is a most encouraging fact, as showing that more and more people are learning to appreciate noble houses and their pictures. They realize perhaps for the first time how full their country is of beautiful things, so infinitely well worth preserving. The shade of PRINCE PUCKLER-MUSKAN, that too persistent pilgrim in the early nineteenth century, when the DUKE too often had the gout and could not show him his treasures personally, must rejoice on the asphodel. The numbers of sightseers are in some instances as surprising as cheering. If the similitude be not too flippant the great houses may be thought of in terms of football leagues. Thus Chatsworth comes unquestionably at the head of the first league with a score of over 264,000. Blenheim seems likely to be second with some 160,000, but it has now been caught and passed by Woburn with a figure hard on 200,000, and that in its first season. Other lovely and famous houses, perhaps not too easily accessible, fall naturally with lower scores into the second league.

43

These figures restore the belief in human nature, because it can never be denied that looking at houses can be a fatiguing task. So, for that matter, can looking at anything to which the looker is unaccustomed, productive of a sudden watering of the eyes and aching of the legs. The unhardened spectator at a picture gallery may often be seen to sink in a weak state on to the central sofa and visitors to houses are sometimes similarly overcome. Students of *Bleak House* will recall the excursion made by Mr. Guppy and his friend Jobling to Chesney Wold. They are " dead beat before they have well begun. They straggle about in wrong places, look at wrong things, don't care for the right things, gape when more rooms are opened, exhibit profound depression of spirits, and are clearly knocked up." A sombre picture and possibly overdrawn but with a gleam of malicious truth. It was characteristic of such occasions that the one thing that Mr. Guppy really wanted to know was the legend of the Ghost's Walk and that was " not related to visitors." It was ever thus. A glimpse of the house's owner hastily escaping into the garden, or even of a lordly mackintosh hanging on a strictly private peg, is sometimes more exciting than the most precious of Old Masters. As the last shutter closes behind the pilgrim emerges into the outer air a little dazed by all the splendours he has seen. His visit may be like that to a spa, when full benefit of the cure, so the doctors say, will only be felt afterwards.

FOCUS ON FREEDOMS

A FOURTEEN-YEAR-OLD schoolgirl, MISS PAT KELD, has been given the freedom of the Billingham-on-Tees public baths for two years ; she earned this enjoyable distinction by bravely rescuing a boy from drowning in a stream. This sensible and imaginative arrangement suggests that freedoms might well be bestowed on a less protocolaire basis than they are at present. Much as we all yearn to be given the freedom of (say) Huddersfield, we know jolly well that such an honour is—to put it as euphemistically as possible—a remote contingency. Our services to the State, though marked by a sort of clueless loyalty tempered by ineffective bouts of anarchism, have not—so far, at any rate—been of a kind to excite the spontaneous gratitude of aldermen ; and on lovely Huddersfield herself all too few of us can claim to have conferred the smallest benefit.

It is true that in this particular sphere most of us look like being—in a phrase used by schoolmasters who, though baffled, are reluctant to admit defeat—late developers. But even if we do develop late, what are we going to do with the freedom of Huddersfield when we get it ? Worn out, as by then we shall be, by our unremitting services to the cause of humanity, what will that *ville lumière* have to offer us ? Even if its legendary night-life attracts us, what guarantee have we that the chuckers-out will be easily persuaded that we enjoy a kind of *droit de Seigneur* at the Palais de Danse ? If our motor-car is left unattended in one of its leafy boulevards, how delicate, perhaps even how bootless, will be the task of convincing the constable who seeks to summon us that he is committing, inadvertently, a solecism ! To be brutally frank, it looks as if the stigma of not having been given the freedom of any city, borough or municipality is one which we shall never have much trouble in concealing behind a façade of insouciance.

There are, however, other freedoms which, had we earned them earlier in our careers, we could have done with. It was freedom from, rather than freedom of, to which we initially aspired ; we wanted to be let off things, rather than let into them. Prayers, ablutions, dancing lessons, finishing up our pudding, putting away our toys, kissing aunts good-night, running along, now, like a good little thing—these were the landmarks which studded the sunlit but seldom attainable uplands of freedom. Later we should have appreciated less negative privileges. Had we, for instance, enjoyed the freedom of the university printing press, we should very probably have got a First ; and unrestricted access to the quartermaster's stores, the right to ride to hounds without subscribing to the pack's welfare, and a free pass to the Memorial Theatre at Stratford-upon-Avon would all have conferred benefits from which we should have gained according to our natures. But it is too late now to dream of guerdons which we never won. It remains only to congratulate MISS KELD, together with the provost and fellows of the Billingham-on-Tees public baths. And, gazing into the future, to try rather wistfully to imagine a situation in which, unaided, we shall rescue the Mayor of Huddersfield from a watery grave.

IN THE MEDICINE CUPBOARD

At some stage in the development of the family the medicine cupboard comes into being. A window sill or the modest shelf above a wash-basin will carry all the bottles that a single person needs to sustain his health, but bring two or more beings together in the same household and it is extraordinary how the bottles multiply. It is rare for a medicine to be quite finished ; for the last measure in the bottle to be poured with a sigh of relief into spoon or tumbler. Somewhere about the half-way mark it is generally deemed either to have served or failed in its purpose and is thereupon abandoned. Therein lies the trouble, for a strange superstition that the malady might return restrains the hand that would otherwise throw the beastly stuff away. At this point the medicine cupboard offers itself as a happy solution, and the bottle, and the cupboard, pass into an oblivion from which they are seldom roused.

The remarks made recently by a medical officer of health are of just the kind to bring them back into the picture. His criticism was not necessarily directed against them. He was deploring the efforts that are often made to persuade people that they are more dead than alive. But his reference to the " fantastic array " of purges and tonics will have tickled the conscience of many who are not normally aware of being hypochondriacs. A visit to the medicine cupboard in this frame of mind can be revealing. Unless the primary object of providing something in an emergency has been kept firmly in view, the cupboard, for all its glycerine and lint, will have taken on the function of a museum rather than a first-aid post. That Mixture in the broad-shouldered bottle stood guard beside the bed of a victim of jaundice two years ago, and that Ointment was applied so long ago that it is difficult to know whether it was designed for a strained ligament or some infantile rash. Next to it a round box bears the name of a nanny who left years ago, and what complaint it was that yielded to those vermilion pills will never again be known. An oleaginous liquid in an unlabelled, fluted bottle is presumably medicinal but looks like bat oil, while some tiny lozenges have clearly only been preserved because of their hideous cost.

There is not much here with which to reproach oneself, except indecision, but a closer inspection may reveal four or five cough cures, as many answers to the common cold—including some infallible remedies from friends that were not convincing—powders to restore the digestion, and tonics to rally a flagging vitality. The medical officer in a memorable passage suggests that " palatable purgatives " might be the first to be thrown into the river. His bold advice may not be followed to the letter, but it might easily lead to a lessening of congestion in the cupboard.

ON PROBATION

"PRISONER at the bar," said the judge in Erewhon, "you have been accused of the great crime of labouring under pulmonary consumption, and after an impartial trial before a jury of your countrymen, you have been found guilty." He thereupon sentenced the poor wretch to imprisonment with hard labour for the rest of his miserable existence, tempered by two daily tablespoonfuls of castor oil. That was a savage penalty, but at this time of year milder ones are often inflicted, not by the High Court but by purely domestic tribunals. The delinquent shows incipient signs of going wrong by a volley of sneezes or by snuffling with felonious intent. He is sentenced to a period of probation. He is ordered to have breakfast in bed next morning and warned of the dire results that will ensue if he fails to behave himself. If there is as much as the suspicion of a temperature, in bed he will stay for the whole day and be dosed, not indeed with castor oil but with ammoniated quinine. This sentence is far from a disagreeable one and perhaps the best part of it is the going to bed on the night before with the blessed knowledge of that long lie next morning. Yet when he is called, the prisoner leaps out of bed far more eagerly than usual in order to wash and shave, not from any enthusiasm for those processes, but in order to snuggle cosily back into bed with the knowledge that they are done for the day and that nothing can mar the next two hours of perfect idleness.

Should the sentence be extended and the prisoner kept in bed for a whole day or even more he may find himself beginning to develop some of the characteristics of a hardened offender. It may be he has been told not to

49

smoke, since it is bad for his sore throat. Like the old lag who secretes tobacco in some crevice in his cell he will seize the moment when his guards have left him to snooze, and make a raid on the box of cigarettes next door. He will certainly be found out, but after all, what can they do to him ? Or again a fine day may even tempt him to break prison, so that he creeps out for a few illicit moments into the sunshine. The passers by will not recognize him as an escaping criminal, but will believe him an ordinary respectable citizen. This is, however, an unwise course, very likely entailing an appearance before the doctor with threats of repulsive medicines. He had far better stay peacefully in bed, enjoying the prison diet, which is very light and wholesome, and the sound of the telephone bell dying away into a petulant silence because he might catch a chill in answering it. These are blessed privileges and the first breakfast in bed is the most regal of all.

WELL

MOST people are familiar with the type of wireless programme in which a panel of half-hearted exhibitionists attempt to answer questions submitted by the audience. The questions may deal with any of the problems which—starkly or lymphatically, evitably or inevitably—confront the community, excepting only such problems as are due for discussion within the next fortnight by the community's elected representatives; these are wisely reserved by our rulers—in rather the same way as a bagged fox or a carted deer—for the occasion regarded by all *bona fide* subscribers to the hunt as most appropriate. Listeners may well have supposed that the great difficulty in a programme of this kind is to induce the participants to stop talking; but there arises (a B.B.C. producer has revealed) a minor but even more intractable dilemma when they start giving tongue. They all, always, begin by saying——" Well."

The huge man hitting a huge gong, the snarling and extravagantly leonine lion, who act as rather meaningless ushers to so many films no longer strike us as particularly interesting; but they have a certain *panache* which the monosyllable " Well " lacks. " The next question comes from Mrs. Eunice Stripe: Does the team believe in original sin and, if so, what would they like to see done about it ? " There is a momentary pause while this searching inquiry, so typical of the more vigorous trends in contemporary thought, is allowed to sink in. Then the questionmaster gathers up the reins in his light, experienced hands and says : " Marmaduke ? " There is another pause. "Well," says Marmaduke ; and launches forth.

What else could he have said ? Broadly speaking, there are two alternatives. He might have said nothing, but plunged straight either into dogma (" There is no such thing as original sin ") or into illuminating reminiscence (" It was in a conservatory, at a hunt ball organized by the Loamshire Otterhounds—how sad that this once fashionable pack no longer exists—that I first, as it were, rubbed shoulders with original sin.") It will be seen at once that either type of opening gambit, though it gains nothing from the " Well " tacked on in front of it, loses a *je ne sais quoi* of artlessness and spontaneity if not so prefaced. Each becomes vaguely unseemly. It is as though boxers had started to fight without shaking hands, duellists without saluting each other. The other alternative to saying " Well " is to say something else instead. " Zounds ! " or " Stap my vitals ! " might, if fed into the stream of broadcasting at a point much nearer its source, have achieved the same meretricious but acknowledged status as the man with the big gong and the lion with (it would seem) slight indigestion. COMMANDER CAMPBELL missed the chance of making "Avast there ! " or even " Shiver my timbers ! " standard usage ; and efforts, however well meant, to wean the oracles from their addiction to a monosyllable which makes them sound at once judicious, informed, self-effacing, well-bred and practically anything else the listeners care to read into it are almost certainly doomed to failure. It will be best for the producers to leave well alone.

VANISHING LORE

THE incurable sentimentalist, the unrepentant praiser and lover of times past, has not to look far to find evidence of change—and, therefore, decay—in the habits and manners of men and the nation. His lamentations, like sprinters crouching on the starting line, are sometimes a little too quick off the mark, but even the most determined and prosaic of modernists will sympathize with him at the news that a spokesman for the farmers of East Anglia has declared that they set such store by the B.B.C.'s television weather forecasts that no longer—and here tare the cause and the matter for tears—do they "forecast he weather by the signs of the countryside.",

Sad it is indeed to think that, as time passes, so will local weather lore, handed down verbally from one generation to another, die out. Soon, too soon, that charming little couplet about the inevitable splash that will result should the oak bud before the ash—or should it be the other way round ?—will be forgotten and to the shepherd red skies at morning will be at one with red skies at night, a spectacle merely, as innocent of warning as of promise. It is not, however, the rhymes and signs known to the townsman as well as the countryman that are so precious ; it is, rather, the scraps of mysterious weather superstitions to be found up and down the land. Each locality has its own favourite omens, and, while one can discern a tempest in the pattern of a spider's web, another can tell by the way a leaf spins to the ground whether anticyclone or depression will prove triumphant. Again, a message written in the hedgerow can be interpreted by one village in a sense that flatly contradicts the verdict given by its neighbour a mile or two down the road.

The best of this falling-out on the part of rustic prophets is that all in the end can generally claim that it was their nap selection which turned up trumps. In spite of the jokes of the professional humorists, ours is a temperate climate, averse from extremes, and, when the perambulations of a snail spell tempest to one and calm to another, the weather generally compromises with a light wind and so allows each school of thought to claim the victory. Rain, too, is difficult to measure and to define in terms of violence. To the cricketer running for the shelter of the pavilion it seems as though the heavens have opened, while the spectator shows by his ironic applause that he regards the fall as merely a sprinkling of a passing shower. Thus the high priest, who, after examining the behaviour of the temple-haunting martlet, has proclaimed a fine day and his rival who has gloomily plumped for a downpour have both a case to put forward. It is, alas, a little too vague and subjective, too endearing and old-fashioned, to hold its own against the bright pictures on the television screen and the assured manner of the scientific expert with his maps and charts showing cold fronts, occluded fronts, isobars, and all the rest of it.

GONE AWAY

BO-PEEP was never, so far as her recorded history tells us, a Mistress of Foxhounds. Had she been, her country would evidently have lain in Kent. The other day a pack got lost there in dense woods near Detling, and their huntsman ruefully remarked that he had never heard of hounds being missing for so long. It was in Kent that, many years ago, a visitor from the Whaddon Chase exclaimed, in the hunting field, " What's the name of this forest ? My huntsman would begin to cry directly we got into such a place, let alone try to hunt a fox." These woodland hazards of the foxhunter will cheer up every owner of a single, mutinous dog—or, more properly, perhaps, of a half couple. The hunting folk, as we pass them on the road, always seem to be almost insolently in control. As they amble along on horseback, surrounded by their dogs, we shudder to think what would happen if all their dogs were like our dog.

But nothing of the sort does happen. A little crackling play with a whip, a few well-chosen words, and the bevy keeps to its own side of the road. We drive past at walking pace and are greeted with a courteous rise of the dog-master's cap. He and the knowing ones who join him at the Meet have two other tricks for which we envy him. He is able, with apparent confidence, to count thirty-one dogs (the number that got lost in the woods) while they are weaving about between one another's heads and sterns with the intricacy and with no little of the grace of ballet dancers. A concentrated gaze, reminiscent of a ship's officer of the watch, is enough to justify him in murmuring : " Fifteen and a half couples ; all on." We try to emulate his feat and make the count, first, twenty-nine, then thirty-three, and thereafter, anyone's guess, because the wretched dogs will keep getting in each other's way.

The second trick (which may, sometimes, be a confidence trick) is won by remarking, nonchalantly, " That Milkmaid is a beautiful bitch, got a nose as good as dear old Priscilla's." The stranger, looking bewilderedly at the milling crowd, can see only one member of it standing out, and he is obviously not Milkmaid. But the knowing ones know and, thinking of that ill-disciplined little half couple at home, whose appearance is only too familiar, the amateur finds his inferiority complex growing like a giant vegetable marrow. So it is nice to be reminded that there is more to foxhunting than is contained in the old sportsman's riddle. " How far can a dog run into a wood ? " the riddle ran, and the answer was " Half way, because after that he is running out." But not, it seems, if the Kentish evidence is to be relied upon, until he feels like it.

SEAMY SIDE UP

"Psst, Mister, want to buy a cricket ball ? " The question sounds improbable, but it may well have been asked in the warm Bengal dusk, as shadowy figures, hands half across mouths, whispered temptation to flannel-clad passers-by. No less than £150 worth of cricket balls, stored for use in first-class matches, were stolen at one fell stroke from the Cricket Association by non-sportsmen of the sub-continent. This bumper haul (at present prices) is yet another reminder of how unexpectedly games exported from this old country may get given new twists in another place. Cricket has for so long basked in the sunshine of impeccable respectability that even the most hard-pressed writers of crime fiction have let it alone.

Here and there, an incident comes to mind from real life or from a story. MR. COMPTON's gear was stolen with his car outside Lord's, but have thieves ever dared to break into the hallowed ground ? If so, they are forgotten and nothing nearer to the true meaning of " not cricket " seems to survive than that lamentable display of ill-temper by the most famous of fictional performers between pavilion and nursery end. What he said will never be known—for only the Eton wicket-keeper heard it and he did not tell—but every fag saw the scowling face of the demon batsman as he retired leaving spread-eagled stumps behind him. Still, he would, probably, have drawn the line at kidnapping the Eton captain's favourite bat and none of the villains who stole examination papers and put watches and wallets into innocent pockets ever stooped to cutting up a pitch or to selling the school's stock of pads on the black market.

57

But, before the Bengal team claims that it has lit a pioneer candle, it should consider the founding fathers of Lord's. Some of them would have bought the whole £150 pile—and sold it again at a profit. Generations of good behaviour on and off the ground have caused their record to grow dusty and neglected. They deserve to be revived, if only to show the crooks of the ancient East that there is nothing new under the sun—not even at cricket. Let us then praise—or at least recall—the betting men who forgathered with the players in the " Green Man and Still " in Oxford Street and—too often successfully—invited them to sell a match. Then, spectators were sometimes privileged to see fielders trying to take the wickets of batsmen who were doing their best to get out. Those were the days in which, at a Lord's Annual General Meeting, two pertinent questions were asked—" Who sold the match at Nottingham ? " and " Who would bowl at anything but the wicket for Kent ? " In that uninhibited atmosphere, with bookmakers calling the odds in front of the Pavilion, LORD FREDERICK BEAUCLERK offering a bribe to have a disagreeable score suppressed and the BISHOP of LONDON forbidding his clergy to take part in big matches, a Bengal spiv, with nothing better to offer than an armful of stolen balls, might have passed unnoticed—or been invited to join the M.C.C.

PARISH PERENNIAL

A POSTER on the vicarage gate, and another on the church notice board, and a few affixed to the trunks of trees, and a dozen or so in house windows announce that the church bazaar has come round again. No event in the church's social calendar recurs with more certain regularity. The main reason is no doubt to be found in those familiar financial difficulties which recur with the same inevitability—if recur be the right word for something that does not come and go so much as haunt the place from basement to belfry from one year's end to the next. The sale of work provides a few cartloads of gravel to cast in the slough of insolvency. But this is not the whole explanation of an ecclesiastical phenomenon. The hymn-books and the hassocks might be in mint condition, the organ free from debt and the rafters clear of beetle, and still it would be necessary to " invent " the bazaar. The parish, and the life of the parishioners, would hardly be the same without it.

There are many men, and some women, who do not like bazaars. Shopkeepers frown on them with understandable suspicion, and mayors and other celebrities have been known to take solemn oaths never to open another. But these are special cases and they would make bad canon law. Bazaars are not intended for their benefit, least of all for the celebrities, who must not imagine (who are not so naive as to imagine, either) that it is merely the pleasure of their company that the vicar is after when he sends them that flattering letter of invitation. The bazaar is to benefit the parish, and incidentally (but not so incidentally as all that) to give all the workers of the church, all the jam-makers and cake-makers and embroiderers, the tenor soloist and the boy soprano, the vicar's warden and the vicar's wife, an occasion for a grand display of their talents and for a great deal of happy bustle. And that goes, as they say, for anyone in the neighbourhood who feels like joining in.

Like the pantomime which in some ways it resembles, the church bazaar adheres to safe traditional paths— and who would have it otherwise ? A new curate will give it a new twist now and then, but broadly it remains as it was fifty years ago, with a great deal of bunting and coloured paper about, and a preserves stall laden with marrow jam and home-made marmalade, and great displays of needlework from the ladies' working party, and a bookstall run by the graver members of the congre-gation, and a cake to guess the weight of, and a concert by the scouts, and teas and suppers (including sausage and mash if the resources of the church hall will permit), and such furious activity, such jostling and cheerfulness and fug as was never seen or heard before in living memory—or at least, not since last year. In many a village and small bleak town, in days of poor communica-tions, before the cinema and the wireless, the sale of work was one of the highlights of the year. Its simple pleasures now have more competitors to meet, but still it seems to hold its own. The posters are up again, at any rate.

LOCAL AUTHOR

AUTHORS have to live somewhere, but they do not in general exhibit the gregarious tendencies noticeable among artists, who are often said to live in colonies. This difference between the two types of creative genius may be something to do with their *geists,* whatever these may be ; or it may simply arise from the fact that artists derive more advantages from propinquity than authors would if they went in for it. The painter and the sculptor use a far wider range of tools and raw materials than the writer does. Nothing in an author's household quite corresponds to the injunction " Pop out and see if you can borrow some gamboge," variants upon which echo intermittently through all save the best regulated studios ; nor does the conception of sharing a model appeal to even the most unoriginal novelist.

Hence it comes that, outside London, authors are distributed in an arbitrary and irregular way throughout our islands, what pest officers call infestations being comparatively rare. Even those who take on a kind of protective colouring and merge into their surroundings are known for what they are. As objects of interest they come below reprieved murderers but above retired admirals. " That's where an author lives," the visitor will sometimes be told ; the amused contempt in his host's voice, as he points out the humble abode, is sometimes qualified by a hint of proprietorial pride. It is on this pride, one imagines, that the bookseller in the local town hopes to trade when, the writer having (slightly to everyone's surprise) actually written a book, the work in question is exhibited in the bookseller's window under a notice saying " By Local Author." It seems to be a sort of law of nature, and a slightly unjust one at that, that we find it impossible to take with complete seriousness literary works by members of our own family or by people whom we know very well; but this lack of *rapport* does not necessarily apply to people whom we know only by sight, and our curiosity about a book may even be whetted by the fact that we once saw the writer changing a spare wheel or taking a pair of shoes to be soled.

But are we in fact more likely to buy a book because it is by a local author? The bookseller, and still more the gifted creature himself, hope that the answer is Yes. Perhaps it is. Tradesmen whose customer the author is would in hard fact be well advised in their own interest to buy his book and thus increase his purchasing power. But if he pays his bills punctually they may shortsightedly conclude that his resources are ample already, and if he does not pay his bills punctually they will regard him as an undeserving citizen whom it is no business of theirs to oblige. As for the ordinary resident, he is quite likely to reflect that a lot of other people in the district are bound to buy the book anyway, so it will be easy for him to borrow it; and in the end the fact that the poor author is local may have no more effect on his neighbours' sales-resistance than if he lived in the south of France. The only way to be quite certain of cashing in on his residential qualifications is for him to write his book about the place he is local to, with plenty of thinly veiled and unflattering portraits of its leading residents. Then it will sell like hot cakes.

DOMESTICATED DUMBO

"HE is not *musth*," the man replied indignantly, "only his honour has been touched. Is an elephant an ox or a mule that he should tug at a trace ? His strength is in his head." So spoke the mahout of the lead elephant deputed to haul the big forty-pounders, and if the elephant felt it beneath him to do such skilled and honourable work—" only a low-caste elephant will pull a gun "—what is to be thought of Dumbo, who has been helping to clear up the leaves at the Zoo ? A photograph has been taken which shows her emptying a basket of leaves into a wheelbarrow, a menial task indeed and one more becoming to an animal lower in the physical and social scale. Either Dumbo, it seems at first sight, must herself be a very common sort of elephant or else deplorably lacking in dignity.

But perhaps there are excuses for her. Maybe she regards the work as the equivalent of what, in a former age, was known as " slumming," as something which appeared to the rich and the privileged as a cross between a duty and a hobby. She may have brought to her leaf-tidying that same air of indulgent patronage which distinguishes a lady of the manor entering into the competitions of the village *fête* taking place in her grounds. It is not too fanciful thus to speculate on Dumbo's motives, for elephants are animals of great intelligence and sagacity. Their memory is, of course, legendary, but there is much more to an elephant's brain than the mere faculty of remembering, an asset traditionally enabling it to pick out indigent friends at the circus and transplant them to more expensive seats. Elephants are kindly and benevolent in their wisdom—what a world of comfortable, homely assurance there is in the word " Jumbo." Indeed, when the matter is pondered, it is not at all difficult to imagine elephants wearing glasses. MR. J. B. PRIESTLEY, when in his dream he encountered the Berkshire Beasts, which were not unlike elephants, found them all wearing spectacles and he goes on to add " I did not see anything very droll in all this." Nor is there any reason why he should ; for elderly, domesticated elephants, spectacles are clearly the thing.

Dumbo may not yet have come to that, and probably the real reason why she helped with the leaves was sheer boredom. It is a far trumpeting from the world of emptying wicker-work baskets to KIPLING'S

An' the elephants bring up the guns !
Ho ! Yuss !
Great-big-long-black-forty-pounder guns,
but both Dumbo and her military ancestors share the need common to all animals in captivity, the need to do something positive and constructive. The leaves of late autumn are now fast deserting the trees and when the last one falls Dumbo, her occupation gone, will have to find something else to which to turn her trunk.

VOLES PREFER COX'S

Animals, it is sometimes alleged, do not reason, and their actions are mere reflexes. It is a sad and arid doctrine, and will be left to the scientists willingly enough by most laymen, who have long ago cherished an opposite view. Our dumb friends, they instinctively feel, may be dumb—indeed by definition they must be so—but they are not so dumb as all that, and any little titbit of animal intelligence is therefore sure of a friendly welcome among humans. The latest news item of the kind comes from Paris in a report of the international body known in French as Oepp and in English as Eppo—or more verbosely as the European and Mediterranean Plant Protection Organization—whose latest publication is an account of the deleterious activities of field rodents during the years 1953 and 1954. Here we read that water voles in Denmark have been doing damage to apple trees—and that they " sometimes show a marked preference " for Cox's orange pippins.

Now the water vole is a charming little beast, whom it is distressing to find in trouble, for he has many talents. To watch the neatness with which he will fell a long shoot of flote grass, by biting it through at the base, and then slowly consume it from one end to the other in a single prolonged nibbling session, is to acquire a high regard for the water vole's workmanlike ways ; and to wonder why the English countryman can be so inept as to call him a water rat. But then, who could blame a mere rustic for a trifling misnomer of that sort when the zoologists—with that deliberately defended and logical obscurantism so characteristic of scientific nomenclature—call the water vole *Arvicola terrestris*—which seems

65

like a denial of his essential nature ? But this is to wander away from the main point, which is that the last thing to be expected of the water vole is that he should prove himself a connoisseur of apples—or at least of apple trees, for it is not the fruit, but the layer under the bark, which he fancies.

At first sight it may strike one as odd that Eppo's (or Oepp's) correspondents report no such fondness for Cox's orange pippins among water voles in England. Perhaps this is only because the sluggish and slow-witted English have not so far noticed it. Yet a better notion comes to mind. England is the country of origin of that particular apple, and can it be that English water voles have, from long acquaintance, tired of it ? If so they would only be falling into line (if quadrupeds can fall into line with bipeds) with many human Britons, who are beginning to feel that, excellent as are MR. COX's orange pippins, may be they are not, or should not be, the only pippins in the orchard. To Danish voles they are, no doubt, still something in the way of delicious novelties. But the true born English water vole—may he not feel that the time has come again for a Blenheim or a Darcy Spice ? That must be it—and the water vole is evidently an even more intelligent beast than Oepp's (or Eppo's) report would suggest.

THE ODD HALFPENNY

LITTLE coins in the pocket, like little men in the street, are perennially threatened by inflation. When they first came, brave and shiny, from the Mint, nothing less than big business deals were good enough for them. One of the few things that some of us remember from our paddling on the beaches of the deep seas of medieval economic history is that there was a demand for land to be sold at fourpence an acre. Nowadays, even a Ministry or a local authority armed with the most enviably wide powers of compulsory purchase would flinch from naming so modest a figure. The groat, or fourpenny bit, has vanished, except as an old-fashioned word of contempt.

Farthings have managed to keep themselves above the counter—but only just. Their uses are restricted. A patron who sought to pay for the cheapest seat at the cinema in farthings would be unpopular with the lady of the box office. The halfpenny alone still finds itself as busily in full employment as it was when they first coined it in silver. Indeed, it is busier, for it makes such a convenient little token of rising prices. A farthing on a bus fare would be more nuisance than it was worth. A halfpenny, at the cost of grumblings from passengers and fumblings for change from conductors, does the trick. It may count itself lucky, and yet it must sigh for the better days it has known. As a First Elizabethan it remembers a quart of ale or beer going for a penny and a " pynte for a hapeney." Much later, and within mortal living memory, a child could exchange it for two ounces or more of sweets that lasted long in the mouth.

The sneers that assailed its humble fellows for their smallness seem largely to have passed it by. On the cup of the refined lady among the Canterbury Pilgrims no farthing was seen of grease. Adventurers in melodrama were warned that—so cunningly had the lawyers tied the money up—they could not hope to touch a farthing from a coveted fortune. Boasters did not care a brass farthing and tarnished reputations were not worth a groat. The halfpenny was seldom put to such invidious uses in print or conversation. It is true that a Shakespearian heroine tore a letter into a thousand halfpence and naughty boys, who ought to have been in church, were known to sit on tombstones playing halfpenny-under-the-hat. But, on the whole, the little brown fellow has avoided bad company. At one point in its strenuous career it showed remarkable ingenuity. Saving hogs by a touch of tar was too homely and rustic a job for it, and, so, it cleverly contrived to promote the flock into a fleet—and, to this day, the ship and not the sheep proverbially suffers from false economy over a halfpenny. Undeniably, here is a coin to be handled with respect on buses.

A PAIR OF BLUE STOCKINGS

ENVY itself will join in cheering the eighteen-year-old schoolgirl who has, within a few hours, had two telegrams offering her open exhibitions. The one was from Cambridge and the other from Oxford, and she has put her money on—or rather decided to take it from—a light blue college. Doubles more memorable may have been brought off. But, in these days of queuing young women, seeking and not finding a niche in the higher educational scheme of things, this does seem to be what DAMON RUNYON would have called " more than somewhat." Never—or so it seems to the sixth formers of seminaries from Cheltenham to St. Leonard's across the Border—have so many been writing papers in the hope of getting placed among so few vacancies.

To have earned the right to pick and choose on this stricken, casualty strewn field is worthy of the pioneers— the old contemptibles in the most honourable sense of the phrase—of the battles of the blue stockings. They were not snugly entrenched, as the girls of to-day are, in prepared positions.

> This is woman's true position—
> In the kitchen's inmost nook ;
> For a lady's noblest mission
> Is to cook.

It was with such rude cries ringing in their ears that MISS RAMSAY and MISS PHILIPPA FAWCETT rounded Cape Turk and sailed past Seraglio Point. But they made their landfalls. MISS RAMSAY was shown, in a cartoon, being saluted, as she entered a First Class carriage, labelled " For Ladies Only," in honour of her having been placed Senior Classic. MISS FAWCETT, although she could not get a degree, was rated officially above the Senior Wrangler.

So the light verse writers had to play a different tune.

> I've spent all my cash on a crammer
> And I'll only get β or γ ;
> But that girl over there
> With the flaming red hair
> Will get α+ easily, d — n her.

What man has had such a tribute paid to him ? Even LOREBURN's impudent double does not seem to have been honoured in verse. Having won a demyship at Magdalen, he asked the President for permission to try his luck for a Balliol scholarship, was naturally and indignantly refused, burnt his boats and got the scholarship. But no Cambridge college wooed him. No man is ever likely to be complimented, as was ELIZABETH CARTER, on being able to make a pudding as well as translate EPICTETUS and work a handkerchief as well as compose a poem. But, no doubt, the lady who has chosen Cambridge can do all those things, and somebody should celebrate her in a limerick.

TWO TUNES ON A DRILL

WHOEVER invented the pneumatic drill was a black magician in the first flight. He might, as he loosed the thing on the world, have shouted gleefully, as Prospero did to *his* Caliban, " Hag-seed, I'll make thee roar, that beasts shall tremble at thy din." Never did so small a gadget have a more fearful voice. It is raised at the moment in every other street. At its command, office windows tremble, and executives in conference cannot make themselves heard. Lying in bed in the morning with half an hour still to go, you are relentlessly roused from a quarter of a mile off. Pass it in the street, with its attendant bowed respectfully over it, guiding its convulsive jerks, and you are well-nigh deafened. And the beauty of it is that, from the angle of the small boy lurking in all of us, there is nothing to be done about it—or so we are told.

Too many vehicles getting themselves jammed on too frail road surfaces make its seasonal performance compulsory. The small boy likes to make noises and messes. The pneumatic drill makes both with complete and unfettered licence. Those who seek to play the same sort of game in other fields find their style at least a little cramped. The open-cast coal miners have to put up with fussy complaints and even, very occasionally, with effective obstruction when they prepare to grub up the green and brown face of the land. The erectors of giant steel stilts are sometimes made to put them away tidily instead of perching them, as they would prefer to do, on the most conspicuous points of down and moor. But the spoil-sports are tongue-tied when faced by the drill. Nobody ever answers it back.

71

Satisfactory though this is to plain, shrewd men who argue that the world cannot stand still and who get tired of the often unreasonable whimpering of lovers of peace, quiet, and beauty, there is another side to it. We pride ourselves on progressively harnessing nature by our infinite resource in mechanical invention. We have put a girdle round the earth and are shortly to put one round space. Undeniably we are clever fellows, and it would be perverse and foolish to point out that, if our ancestors in their sailing ships had made a landfall in a South Sea island and heard a pneumatic drill at work, they would have assumed that the natives worshipped an unusually revolting idol. All the same, it will be nice if, when we make our landfall on the moon, we find the mooncalves prodding their craters with a noiseless drill. That—so the reactionary types among us suspect—is about the most that we can hope to get out of the moon.

HERE, LET ME TRY !

Is there a household in which the familiar remark, indicating that someone else is being frustrated by a lid, has not been heard in the past few days ? A problem from which we are never far removed has been aggravated by the seasonal influx of strange containers sealed with a thoroughness that would be praiseworthy if it were not exasperating. The science of opening lids has not kept pace with the science of closing them, a truth which the host has plenty of time to consider as he crouches, his features suffused by a dull purple, over a jar of crystallized pomegranates from a friend in Beirut. Help is, of course, at hand. "Here, let me try !" and no sooner has reluctance to admit defeat been overcome than another figure is writhing about the room with the cause of the trouble clutched to a crumpled waistcoat. He is moved to these extraordinary antics by the best of motives, that of helping his neighbour, but is there not also in his motive the ghost of a desire to score off him ?

Physical strength does not count for much among adults. The weight-lifter, the pugilist, even the Rugby forward come in for as much banter as any other sections of the community. The " I-am-the-king-of-the-castle " attitude to life with its muscular emphasis so dear to children does not survive long in adolescence ; and yet sometimes in later life a shadow of it seems to glide over the scene. Sooner or later the adult will stop and try one of those test-your-strength machines, or he will pull himself up to a beam or to the branch of a tree. His reluctance to allow anyone to help him carry heavy loads is a manifestation of the same deep-rooted tendency. So is, surely, the eagerness with which he offers to unscrew tops.

Women have so consistently failed to gain access to the bottled plums that they have lost their pride in the matter. They hand the problem over with hardly any fuss to the man, and very prettily they can do it. But among strangers and in company a sense of rivalry is often hardly concealed. This rivalry is not confined to muscular types. The mild, the flabby, and even the puny get a foothold in the contest, usually on the ground that " there is no use forcing it ; you have to know the knack." The knack having failed, recourse is had to the dodge. The stubborn pot is surrounded by a damp cloth, plunged into cold water, tapped with a blunt wooden instrument, or otherwise forced to submit. The jar always loses in the end, and the oriental delicacy, or whatever it may be, is revealed. Crumpled clothing is smoothed out, cuffs are re-shot, mislaid napkins and glasses are recovered, and seats are resumed. Life goes on as before, except that each one harbours the secret regret that he has not been able, without so much as a grimace or a contortion, to loosen the lid's grip and hand the jar back with the faintest of smiles to an admiring hostess.

A WALLET FOR OBLIVION

For every hundred people who know OWEN WISTER'S *The Virginian* there seems to be only one who has come across *When West Was West*. Yet those who have not The Right Honourable the Strawberries and Colonel Steptoe McDee among their acquaintances are missing a great deal. But it is *At the Sign of the Last Chance*—the closing story in the book—that comes appropriately to mind on this particular morning. It tells how, in one of the ghost towns, lingering on in the far west where once had been the frontier, now long since overrun, the grey-bearded survivors from the local saloon follow the old English custom of burying the inn sign—an acknowledgment that trade and life have gone. In some similar mood do we take down the calendars, close up our diaries, and package another bundle of memories on New Year's day. Life is by no means over, but the past is past, and we are moving on elsewhere.

It is a moment for gentle melancholy. Fully granting that it is an old heart that cannot look forward, poor indeed are those who dare not look back. Nor is our pleasure spoilt by the fact that we do so with a certain sadness. GEORGE SAINTSBURY used to dwell on the pleasure of recalling things old and bitter and yet sweet. And while it is no doubt right to greet the future with a smile, only the completely unimaginative or unfeeling would say farewell to the past with a guffaw. Whether it has been better or worse than usual, or the mixture precisely as before, the closing year is now an acquaintance from which we are parting with the certainty that, except

75

in recollection, we can never meet it again. Each one of us will store his or her memories in a different way.

Time hath, my lord, a wallet at his back,
Wherein he puts alms for oblivion.

But, artificial an affair as the calendar is, we have a feeling that in some undefined way to-day is our last chance to treat the happenings of this year as contemporaries. To-morrow the sign will be buried ; a new year begun ; the events, emotions, and impressions of the old quickly overlaid.

HESIOD said Cerberus had fifty heads. We wonder whether it should not rather have been one, or fifty-two, or three hundred and sixty-five. For in a way we are perpetually at the gates of yesterday ; letting in people, and experiences, and strokes of good and bad fortune, that can never emerge again except as shades. This adds to the richness of life as well as to its regrets. Past bearing, even for the happiest, would be the actuality of living in an unending, unchanging present. DR. JOHNSON's friend from Pembroke College became famous because, having tried to be a philosopher, cheerfulness would keep breaking in. Equally, the perpetually cheerful are the better for a little philosophy, even though it may rather damp the proceedings. At the first stroke of Big Ben to-night we can put these thoughts aside and toast the future to our hearts' content. But until then there is no harm in enjoying a little regret.

DAILY DOZE

MEN are far from being agreed, either in theory or practice, on the afternoon nap—on its virtue or otherwise, on whether it should be confined to ten minutes or continue for three-quarters of an hour or be avoided like hashish, on whether it should be taken sitting or flat or taken out of a man's diary altogether. These divisions, however, do not appear until middle life. In the long, preceding years of indiscretion the question does not arise, or arises in a different manner.

At the start, in the very early stages of their development, men take on the whole the naps decreed for them. They could hardly do anything else ; lovingly plied with good food and firmly pinioned in the pram in some sunny spot, they are scarcely in a position to resist the advance of slumber. This phase is quickly followed by another in which, the free spirit of man beginning to assert itself, they refuse increasingly to take life lying down. Gradually the awakening individual finds it possible to stay awake all day, and as babyhood passes into boyhood and boyhood into young manhood it becomes a point of honour to stay up half the night as well. It may be that " life is one long process of getting tired," but no one takes any notice of that sort of nonsense until the process is about half complete. The idea of " lying down " in the middle of the day, or painstakingly " resting " in the parlour, is rightly repugnant to all healthy young humans, and if one of them is in fact " caught napping " now and then it must be after some marathon effort of the field or the study—or of an exacting social life. He is not taking a nap ; the nap has taken him.

Some men retain much longer than others the scorn of an afternoon snooze. Some indeed retain it to the very end, firmly maintaining that night is the proper time for sleep and that dozing in the daytime is a wicked waste of fleeting time. The rest discover in the forties or the fifties or the sixties, or are discovered by, this institution of a nap after lunch. They may not be able to take it daily, because of higher duties, but on Sunday afternoons by the fire in winter, or on Saturday afternoons in a deckchair on the lawn in summer, and on working days when circumstances permit, they drop off to sleep for a brief session. Some of them seek sheepishly to explain themselves ; the doctor ordered it or digestion demands it ; or, they say, they are not really sleeping, but conscientiously relaxing with the eyes closed, and that deep and rather noisy breathing is part of the treatment. Other men have thought it out more carefully and rationalize more boldly ; ten minutes after lunch, they have discovered, adds an hour to the working day, and soon, they infer, you will see them tearing through the office again like a hurricane. But the truest addicts are neither bold nor sheepish ; they simply like the feeling of slipping off into slumber and the feeling of refreshment afterwards ; they are not sensible of any need to cushion themselves with arguments either specious or ingenious ; they are scarcely conscious, as they settle down in the best armchair, that anyone might think they are wasting time—scarcely conscious, scarcely conscious, and soon not conscious at all.

WORMS TO THE RESCUE ?

THERE used to be an element of drama in economics. Slumps occurred ; there were runs on banks ; great enterprises went suddenly bankrupt, and financial wizards jumped off the poops of their yachts leaving (if literate) notes explaining that they proposed to end it all. Pundits spoke of an economic blizzard, and the ordinary man, though quite unable to understand what was happening let alone why, felt vaguely like King Lear. All that seems to have changed now. Things go quietly, almost dreamily, from bad to worse ; our national economy, like a tipsy, remorseful reveller descending an endless, ill-lit spiral staircase, slowly if not very surely makes it progress towards universal ruin without exciting wonder or surprise.

Sometimes this progress is momentarily halted, or even reversed, as the drunkard steadies himself by clutching the balustrade or, reeling, involuntarily reascends a step or two. Then there is talk of a boom ; prosperity assert the pundits, is round the corner. But soon wages are chasing prices again (or is it the other way round ?) and the national economy resumes its shuffle towards the abyss. The ordinary man, bored and bewildered by the whole thing, sees pretty clearly that only some colossal and unforeseen windfall can arrest the lamentable process, and dreams of the discovery of oil in Shropshire, of fabulous diamond mines in Skye, or uranium deposits at Towcester.

His (the ordinary man's) lacklustre eyes must have brightened at the latest news from Aberdeen. Worms ! Why had nobody thought of worms before ? Five million American anglers (a high proportion of whom, it may be assumed, are millionaires) urgently require these humble

79

invertebrates as hook-fodder; a firm in Ohio has approached the Aberdeen Chamber of Commerce in the matter; and plans are already in hand to muster one hundred worm-charmers for night duty on golf courses, parks, and open spaces. At last drama has returned to economics. " The project," the Secretary of the Aberdeen Chamber of Commerce has said, " bristles with difficulties." It is only right that this should be the case. The fact that, as a worm-exporting country, we lack experience is a challenge rather than a drawback. The intrepid cowboy, with his lasso and his great hat, is, after all, a comparative newcomer, the member of a self-made profession. Is there any reason to doubt that the wormboy, rounding up his elusive prey on the moonlit Caledonian greens, will acquit himself less well? America needs twenty-five million worms every year; the ordinary man can see light at the end of the tunnel.

But behind the ordinary man—so clueless, so mirage-prone, so disarming—stalks the dread, desiccated figure of the thoughtful reader, the connoisseur of repercussions, the implication-monger. To him (or to her) the whole concept of international worm-traffic appears to raise wide and controversial issues. To whom, in the first place do these worms belong? They are not covered by the Game Laws; to argue that they represent some form of mineral rights is specious. Why have they not been nationalized? What about open-cast worming? If this great untapped source of national wealth is going to solve our problems, it is surely wrong that only the ruthless and licentious worm-kings should benefit from so lucrative a trade. But how lucrative will it be? If these tiny ambassadors of good will come up to the expectations of their purchasers, the rivers of Ohio will soon be de-populated and the bottom will fall out of the worm-market. By that time we may well have the makings of a civil war on our hands. One or two of the more conventional worm-kings may feel that decorum demands some form of yacht-borne hara-kiri. But in seeking a solution to his immediate problems the ordinary man—like, for that matter, the ordinary fish—had probably better not repose too much confidence in worms.

G

THE NEW FLAG

TO anyone who retains any of the more exciting
tastes of childhood the coming into the world of
another flag must be an event. On January 1, 1956,
there was hoisted the new flag of the Sudan, a fine tri-
colour of blue, yellow and green stripes. These have,
we are told, a symbolic meaning, blue for the Nile,
yellow for the desert, and green—this seems a little bit of
a comedown from a poetical standard—for agriculture.
To people having minds warped by a game these might
appear good colours for a golf club, the green signifying
the fairway, the yellow the sands of the bunker, and the
blue the waters of the engulfing burn; but this may
smack of frivolity and flags are not frivolous; they are
solemn, beautiful and romantic things. In the last forty
years or so, so many countries may be said to have
become other countries that there is probably a considerable crop of new flags; but to those who studied
them while lying on their stomach, as shown on the page
at the end of the big atlas, called " Flags of all nations,"
there are no flags like the old ones. The atlas constituted
perhaps a special treat, only allowed on days so wet
that even a walk was impossible, and the question " What
shall I do next ? " growing ever more urgent, imperatively
demanded an answer. The book's home was on a piece
of furniture mysteriously called a whatnot, in a corner
of the drawing-room fenced by a sofa, and the extracting
of it heightened the anticipation of delight.

There is a grand austerity about the best flags, as there
is about the best coats of arms. They are " simply and
severely great." Nothing indeed could have been plainer
than two flags, the thought of which still makes the

82

heart to throb, those of red and green carried by the herald of the traction engine, which followed him evoking and thundering down the lane. This same simplicity belonged in rich measure to the various tricolours, red, white and blue ; red, white and green ; and red, black and gold. Plain red and yellow stripes were likewise very lovely. Patriotism naturally exacted an affection for the Union Jack, but in the secret recesses of the heart there lurked a feeling that it was too complicated for perfect beauty. Stripes were the thing, and the brighter the better. Indeed, it was a distinct disappointment, when Ivanhoe was first read aloud, to find that the pennons that fluttered so bravely over the pavilions of knights challengers at the tournament were merely of sober russet and black. When there was so much crimson and gold about it seemed that they might have done better than that. The Sudan has done much better ; the new flag is worthy of that sacred page in the atlas.

THE BABIES' LEAGUE

THE correspondent who every year faithfully reports on the names of children announced on our first page has contributed yet another masterly analysis. In a sense, through no fault of his, it is just a little dull. It is natural to hope for a sudden leap up the table by some new favourite, such as the Peters and Michaels, Jennifers and Jeremys achieved a good many years ago. But this time the fine, old, stodgy names, if in a moment of disappointment one may so call them, stay in a firm block at the top. John (a natural, born leader), David, James and Charles have not changed places since last year. To adopt the language of the Eights or the May races, there has not been a single bump among the first four boats. Among the girls it is true there has been one noteworthy downfall ; Mary is now only second on her river, having been caught by Ann and Anne, but it may be argued that such a combination is hardly sportsmanlike Now if Jane had bumped Mary, and she is but a little way behind her, that would have been a fair and honest victory.

It is rather towards the last few places in the list of ten that exciting things happen. Later in the winter we should inevitably have to change our metaphor and think in terms of those promotions and depositions which will then so profoundly agitate the football leagues. William and Robert, for instance, have lost their places in the first league, but that descent can be but momentary. They correspond to such old, heroic names as Blackburn Rovers and Derby County, now in eclipse but bound, as all true romantics must hope, to rise again. On the other hand, Amanda was clearly a rather pedantic flash in the pan and so was Louise ; they could not hope to hold

84

their places for long in the solid unimaginative company of the Sarahs and Carolines. Whether Nicola, now climbing into prominence, will share their fate remains to be seen. Not very long ago Nicola was little more than a *pis aller* when the baby refused to be of the right sex. Someone was inspired to recall a great aunt Nicola and the exchange was made accordingly.

To-day Nicholas appears to be slumping and Nicola booming and Simon and Mark are on the upward surge, though not yet in the first league ; but among the names which must be described as " fancy," Clare, and a very pretty name it is, has achieved that supreme distinction. It may well be that in the walks of life where christenings are not announced in *The Times* but rather in the Parish Magazine, other and more dashing names are favoured. Ivy may not be so popular as of old, but Doreen still has its vogue and Gillian is creeping up. And among the boys Derek holds imperial sway. That delightful essayist " The Londoner," on some points a precise and arbitrary gentleman, once complained of the number of Dereks. It was all very well, he said, for Keppels and Bentincks and those who had come over with Dutch William ; otherwise it was an anomaly and not far from an outrage. But parents will not be dragooned and our perambulators are still full of Dereks.

THE TOWN HALL

THE ordinary citizen, whether of no mean city or the meanest little borough, is not consciously aware on most days of the year of the town hall. He knows that a captain-mayor is ever on the bridge and a pilot-clerk at the helm ; that aldermen and councillors pace ceaselessly the deck ; that stripped to the waist in the engine room are lesser but indispensable men, faithfully serving the ship of local state. The drains, the elm disease, the ducks in the park, the dustbins—they see to everything, all as part of the service, part of " the poetry of things going right," and the ordinary ratepayer rarely gives them a thought. He does not think very often either of the town hall itself—the hub, the nerve centre, the heart of things. He knows the buses start at the side of it, and he must not park his car in front of it, and strangers must turn right at it to reach the public library. He glances at the clock in its tower in passing, and he has learnt that if he hears it strike in the night there may be rain (or something) in the morning. He is dimly aware that the building is there, but it has been there so long that he forgets it. Only at times of crisis does he go inside it. Then he calls to see how much they have put on his ratable value.

Most men are unmoved by such visits, or moved perhaps only to crossness, but a few are surprised into sentiment. It brings back to mind their first impressions of the first town hall they knew. They did a conducted tour of it, perhaps, in a school class taking " civics," and looked down with some awe from the public gallery on the council itself in session. The council now might not impress them greatly, but it appeared to them then a most august assembly. And more impressive even than the council was the splendour of the chamber in which the council sat, and of the mayor's parlour, and the marble staircase, and the stained glass, and the massed chrysanthemums in the entrance hall, and all the light and warmth of the place. Town halls are lost in the largesse of London, but in some grim and grimy little towns they were almost the only secular buildings of any pretensions at all before the super-cinemas came. They might not be the work of architectural genius; it was more often a cause for thanksgiving than for regret that soot and smoke had obscured their choicest detail; but they did give to the eye of youth a glimpse of something that was more than mean and economical and merely utilitarian. The cinemas do that now, sometimes with more taste and frequently with less, both in their foyers and on their screens; and another year or two of television will make every family familiar with all the noblest buildings in the land. But before the first war it was different. It was the town hall then that often represented, for impressionable youth, the civilized and civilizing arts; and who will dare say that it was all a delusion?

MYSTERY MEN

WHO are they ? Sometimes they gaze directly at us across their well-appointed desks. On the wall behind them an Old Master or perhaps a huge graph, steeply, irresistibly ascendant. We are alone with them. "To you, probably," they are saying, "Blenkiron & Moxby's Tubeshafts don't mean a great deal." The rest of the caption explains, in smaller type, that this is a regrettable state of affairs, by which we are the losers. At other times the camera seems to have caught them unawares. They are looking skyward and turning up the collar of a faultlessly cut overcoat : "For Men of Discrimination, This Winter, the New Middleweight Raglan." Sometimes there are two or three of them together (if three, one belongs to a younger age-group). They have glasses in their hands, and grave, judicious expressions on their faces. "The People who Count," says the caption, "Drink Old Spud, the whisky with Stamina."

Yes, but who *are* these Men of Discrimination, these People who Count ? They have, nowadays, an air of solid worth rather than of distinction. Their clothes are good rather than elegant. They wear horn-rimmed spectacles rather than monocles. They are anonymous, but give the impression of having short, yeomanly names like Jenks and Todd. Their neighbours in the other advertisements are mostly female, and a good deal younger. Sometimes the identity of these ladies is revealed ; "Modelled by Flavia Elphberg," it says under the photograph, and the more successful ones get their names into the gossip-columns, when they are described as "top models."

In America this sometimes happens to the men, but not here. Moreover, while there is almost no limit to the number of hats, slacks, ball-gowns, nightdresses, and hacking jackets whose merits the shapely Miss Elphberg can—if necessary all on the same page—help to set off, the Men of Discrimination seem to enjoy much more limited opportunities. What, for instance, is the future of the sincere, grey-haired executive who explained to us what splendid things Blenkiron & Moxby's Tubeshafts were ? Will not the reputation of all these artefacts suffer if, a few weeks later, he appears in a pink coat with a great beaker of port in his hands or, gripping a brief-case, is seen glancing with studied negligence over his shoulder as he enters a huge aeroplane bound for South America ? What does he do when he is not making his necessarily brief appearances before the camera in a Middleweight Raglan ? Apart from the young ladies, who are not really in the same line of business, he has rivals in the shape of real live people—celebrities who explain why they are forever giving each other ballpoint pens, using some unguent, or reading the newspaper of their choice. But these, with all due respect to them, lack the aura of mystery which surrounds the Men of Discrimination. Perhaps—since it goes without saying that they all read *The Times*—one of them will oblige by dispelling it ?

BUT SOFT ! FURNISHING

DESPITE the whimsies of the comic joke gentlemen the big business man's office is an intensely masculine retreat. The outer purlieus may teem with young women. Tea-time gossip, fashion, small talk, even the click of knitting needles may alternate with that of the type-writers. They do not cross the threshold. In the innermost recesses of the glazed brick and mahogany (or cement and chromium) hive, life is real and earnest. Excitements there may be, but they are of a dour and stern order. They bring their satisfactions. But no one would rate among them gaiety, or fantasy, or colour.

All this changes, however, when the Napoleon of Commerce, or even the Murat of Merchandise, decides to have a new office. For him alone, certainly, are such trivialities as the choice of his desk, and the placing of his bells, buzzers, time-pieces, telephones, and television set. But there is one overriding, fundamental, and all-important question he cannot, poor man, decide. That is what colour the place must be. Suddenly he senses a new watchfulness on the part of his secretaries. His working surroundings take on a magnetic attraction for his family. " Have you decided on your carpet, dear ? " (this from his wife) ; " Do you wish me to have your present curtains transferred, sir ? " (secretary). " I say old chap, is it really true you're having pink walls ? " (colleague). Let him answer as light-heartedly as he likes, it is borne in on him these things have become Issues. Like all the higher decisions, moreover, they get themselves inextricably entangled into one issue. " Orange walls and a violet carpet ! Oh no ! You *can't* have that." If he gets these two things right, then the curtains are impossible. What he meant, napoleonically, should take three minutes of his sublime attention he now finds absorbing most of his waking hours. Shade cards accompany the toast at breakfast ; his office is invaded by women trailing lengths of this and microscopic cuttings of that. Something the size of a postage stamp is dropped on the floor and he is asked to envisage it carpeting a vast area. Various bits of card, all looking like putty, are placed against the walls and he is told that of course he can see they won't go with the postage stamp. He stays up late at nights to change his mind for the seventh time on the seventieth permutation and then has to get up early in the morning to do it all over again because " you can't see colours by artificial light, anyway."

Should he attempt, in a furious access of strength, to wash his hands of the whole affair, and say he will just walk into whatever is chosen when it is ready, then he is branded a weakling. Should he stoutly defend some choice of his own, the women's looks at each other clearly tell him he is a fool. No matter. All is really for the best. He may be paying a high price for it, but the fact is he is making his womenfolk thoroughly happy ; cementing a bond between home and office which would be the admiration of any Private Relations Officer ; and, incidentally, ensuring he does get the right thing in the end.

U-HEALTH

"THE Duchess, looking very fit and well . . ." There is something obscurely challenging about these words, which occurred recently in the gossip column of one of the glossier periodicals. On a superficial reading they would seem to represent a straightforward case of tautology ; but anyone whose ear is attuned to the nuances of gossip-column usage will be aware that this is not so, that there is in fact a subtle difference between looking fit and looking well. It is not, however, at all easy to establish what this difference is.

Nobody, in these sort of contexts, has ever been said to look healthy. "The Duchess, I thought, was looking very healthy." What a ridiculous sentence ! What a dreadful way to write about a lady ! *Mens sana,* no doubt, *in corpore sano* ; but one would not dream of describing the Duchess as "looking very sane"—it would sound terribly rude. The same sort of inhibitions prevent one from saying that she looked healthy. Perhaps a clue to our problem is to be found in the phrase "bronzed and fit." Nobody has ever looked bronzed and well, and there is no doubt that in the gossip column "fit" carries with it some of the strenuous, out-of-door undertones which it has upon the sporting page. In hard fact most of the people who appear at cocktail parties and first nights looking bronzed look that way because they have spent the last few weeks lying flat on their backs on a beach and eating and drinking far too much ; the implication that they are trained to the last ounce and ready to run a mile in four minutes is wide of the mark. But then after all they are only said to *look* fit.

There is possibly a slight *double entendre*—of the nicest kind—in a gossip-writer's mind when he or she says that a lady looks well ; the monosyllable conveys a hint of outer radiance as well as the assurance of inner health. It is certainly true that " fit " often does duty alone when applied to men, who tend to play a rather subsidiary and sheepish role in gossip columns (*cf.* " Lady Bisque, who had brought her husband with her "). In this context the epithet probably comes in pretty useful. No male guest at a private view or a musical *soirée* minds reading afterwards that he looked very fit. It may not be absolutely true ; but it is much better than saying that he looked dejected, bored and irritable, and gossip-writers must be allowed some discretion in describing the gay scenes they frequent.

BUS IN URBE

THE differences between central London and the country, never very difficult to detect, emerge at their starkest on a bus ride—a simple bus ride in the country, a sophisticated, complicated, maddening bus ride in the town. In the country—the real country—the journey may still be a neighbourly affair. You know the driver and the conductor and most of your fellow passengers, and they know you, and though this has its disadvantages, it does make for cheerful journeys. There is a general exchange of gossip among the travellers, who may or may not follow the conductor's beat as the chorus swells. It is inconceivable that the driver should ignore the stop where one of his regular passengers is accustomed to get off or another is waiting to get on ; and so far from chafing at the unhurried ritual of greeting that goes with each picking up and setting down, he plays a leading part in it. And between the stops he bowls along quite briskly, unhindered by traffic lights and traffic jams.

How different in the great city, as different as the scenery! Paradoxically, the passenger is more likely to take notice of the scenery in the centre of the town than he is in the country ; he has more opportunity. One of the best ways of seeing London, they used to say, is from the top of a bus, and if seeing London means the minute inspection of the upper storeys of a departmental store from a bus wedged outside it by the press of traffic, then the saying is as true as ever it was. In one sense, too, there are fewer distractions in the bus in town to take the traveller's eye from the scenery ; he is not likely to find himself engaged in a free-for-all debate on parish politics. There will be cheerful chatter between this pair of shoppers and

94

that pair of schoolboys, but a great many of the passengers will be travelling solo, and they will be looking at newspapers or staring stonily out of the window or at each other. They are not stony really, but that is how it looks. They quickly soften into laughter when a Cockney conductor is in the mood to make them, but that does not happen on every bus.

It happens most regularly, in some men's experience, on the buses that travel through the night. This is where the twain of town and country meet. London reverts to the country quite readily in some ways, and the buses of central London can be singularly rural in the early hours of the morning. The passengers are not exactly rural types, but they do know one another. They catch the same bus every night, and on some routes it has always the same driver and conductor, and it has been known to wait for a regular customer who was a few seconds late at his customary stop. The travellers for the most part are those who work late—taxi men returning from the evening's rounds ; waiters from the restaurants ; middle-aged ladies in black, of determined respectability, with an aura of cooking about them ; the odd musician, and men from the newspapers—with a sprinkling of late revellers for variety. It is a dull night on which the bus does not rattle with cheerful gossip. The conductor " at ease " as he is not in the day time, and as the bus leaves the central areas behind and gradually gives up its briefer passengers he is not above making a dent in regulations and sitting down to chat with the regular clients who remain. Nor is the driver cut off from all enjoyment. He gets a cheerful " good morning " from old friends alighting ; and as he get out of range of too frequent traffic lights and away to the sleeping suburbs, he can bowl along quite briskly, just as he would in the wilds.

NO HARD FEELINGS

SHIPS apart, there is a suspicion of affectation about giving a feminine gender to inanimate objects. The remark " She is a beauty," which may very well be applied to a yawl, strikes a jarring note when the subject of the conversation is, for example, a lawn-mower. There are exceptions among cars. The practice is smiled upon in the case of ancient cars, and in the wartime army B echelon was filled with Daisys and Ivys ready to bring up the rations and ammunition. These exceptions reinforce the general impression that man has more affection for his car than he has for his wireless set or his refrigerator, or the other pieces of machinery with which he surrounds himself. Unmistakable though this sentiment is, it begins to wear a little thin at the time of year when batteries show signs of stress and the towing rope is as busy as the plumber.

Happy, and rare, is the driver who has not, at some time or another, listened to the life ebbing from his battery, and had to emerge from his seat wielding a starting-handle. It is difficult to know which suffers more on these occasions, comfort or dignity. Hat, overcoat, muffler, and gloves are worn for a job that should really be tackled in shirtsleeves, and even bending down to look under the car becomes, when one is so dressed, something of an undertaking. Swinging the handle has lost some of the fears it used to hold of broken thumbs and sprained wrists and it does get the circulation going, but it is a difficult exercise to carry out with any dignity and it is extraordinarily dishevelling.

If anything is more undignified than cranking a car it is the next stage, pushing it along the road towards the nearest slope, while others glide by eyeing the pusher, or so he is ready to believe, with scorn in their hearts. The sickeningly gentle free-wheel to the foot of the slope in a silence broken occasionally by an excruciating rending of gears completes the driver's mortification and nearly exhausts the store of good will he has for the vehicle. The mood passes. Something—the G.B. plate, perhaps, or the moments of reflection before help arrives—reminds him that for most of the year his trust in " her " was well repaid. Without fuss she carried her human cargo safely over the Sierra Nevada, bounced musically but intact over Flemish cobblestones, or waited patiently her turn to overtake lorries on the Great North Road. The self-same car caught trains for him, carried all his luggage, sheltered him from winds, and when his feet ached at the end of a tiring day bore him smoothly home to a hot bath. Cold, late, and dirty he may be now, but that is hardly sufficient grounds for severing diplomatic relations. It hardly occurs to him in this forgiving mood that his present distress is in all probability his own stupid fault.

H

MISS GREEK GODDESS, 1956

WHO will be surprised to learn that, on Beverley Hills, the Olympus of California, a Hungarian-born actress has been chosen as the most perfect living example of a Greek goddess ? Anything goes in and around Hollywood and a Paris in those parts needs a whole basketful of golden apples if he is to keep pace with his duty of handing out prizes to Miss Space Traveller, Miss Mother's Day, and the rest. But what is surprising about the latest task of selection with which he has been faced are the qualifications that, on Beverley Hills, are considered to add up to a composite figure of Hera and Aphrodite. She must have classical beauty and stature— that goes without saying. The clear-cut profile and the well-proportioned limbs of the games mistress are, as every schoolboy knows, perquisites of the ladies of old Olympus. But the winner on this occasion had to come first for wit and charm. That should be worth a laugh in whatever quiet backwater of the next world is now the favourite club of the Greek gods. They will have, no doubt, many nice things to say about their ladies. But it passes imagination that any one of them from Zeus to Hermes, would claim that any goddess was witty and, if a case could be made for charm, then SOCRATES would have to steer the argument. Lovely indeed the divine ladies were—" flashing-eyed " like Athene or " white-armed " like Hera herself. But how domestically difficult they were, how less than witty and charming on their mountain home. As ACHILLES once said, when he was at cross-purposes with two goddesses at once (a not unusual predicament for heroes) " needs must a man observe the words of you twain, how wroth soever he be at heart, for so it is better."

How often, if unconsciously, his words must have been echoed, with anguished sincerity, in Hollywood. Looking back on the classics is to be persuaded that the goddesses would have been in their element as film stars. They have the touch. If the Greeks had had the words for it, they would have been known as " tough babies." Take, for example, that marriage, in the highest Olympian circles, which Chelone, a rash young woman, alone refused to attend and at which she mocked. She was turned into a tortoise and condemned to perpetual silence. That was a piece of practical wit to appeal to all goddesses. Still, one must be fair to them. Witty and charming they certainly were in comparison with the Wagnerian goddesses of the north.

THE DRESSING GOWN

THOSE who are in the pleasant stage of convalescence from influenza or other similar ailments have lately perhaps been allowed a distinct step forward. They may sit up for an hour or two by the fire in a dressing gown. In doing so they may have wondered whether that garment, at once so comfortable and so decorative, enjoys quite its ancient splendour. Doubtless it can be acquired, at a price, as floral, as quilted, as generally magnificent as ever it was, but its use is more restricted to practical purposes. Men do not loll in it so superbly as we gather they once did. Sherlock Holmes must have been one of the last of those dressing gown loiterers, who habitually got up by stages. When Watson took the unfortunate engineer, who had just had his thumb cut off, to Baker Street, " Sherlock Holmes was, as I expected, lounging about his sitting room in his dressing-gown." It was the same when the Doctor found him deep in thought over Mr. Henry Baker's old hat ; he was again lounging and this time the dressing gown was purple. It would be easy to amass " parallel instances " ; enough that when the waxen image, made at Grenoble, was put in the window as a trap for Colonel Moran, one of Holmes's old dressing gowns was draped round it to give greater verisimilitude. It may be that there are still left a few of these deceptive loungers who will in an instant fling off the dressing gown for the frock coat and pursue a suspect hansom down Baker Street, but it is to be feared that they are a vanishing race.

If so they are the inheritors of a fine tradition from one who had himself inherited it. Some of the earlier wearers of dressing gowns were glorious creatures such as Mr.

Harry Foker. His was of crimson, if memory serves, and he wore with it a fez or tarboosh. The young men in *Frank Fairleigh* were dressing gownsmen one and all. Yet it must be owned that there were others whose dressing gowns were signs not of genuine opulence, but rather of a shoddy, rakish, vagabond smartness such as would discourage anyone at first sight from lending them even " the ridiculous amount of eighteen pence." Mr. Mantalini almost certainly wore a dressing gown ; so, we have a shrewd suspicion, did Mr. Smangle and Mr. Tigg ; so did half the denizens of the Fleet Prison until they had to pawn them. It could be at once the most ducal and the most disreputable of garments.

If it be true that the dressing gown has slightly but quite perceptibly come down in the world, it is interesting to speculate as to the cause. It may be merely the universal hardness of the times, which puts the old gorgeousness out of reach, but a more likely cause is the coming of pyjamas. They have a dignity and a security that the nightgown could never afford. When poor Mr. Winkle found himself stranded in a high wind, with ladies coming down the crescent, the wind, we are told, took the dressing gown in a most unpleasant manner. Had he been clad in pyjamas he would have been relatively as bold as brass ; but a gentleman in a nightgown presents to the unfeeling eye a mildly ridiculous spectacle.

ALIAS PUSSY

Not much originality is shown in the names that are given to household cats. The pampered pet sitting primly before the fire is probably either Timsy Boy or Tootles. There is Snowball for the white ones and Nigger for the black—in the Services it is usually the other way round, for the same reason that people under five foot eight get called Lofty—while for the " harmless, necessary cat " for which no one in the family has any time and which spends much of its life on outside window-ledges, there are pedestrian names like Tinker and Tiger. Sometimes a flippant or largely irrelevant choice, such as Diogenes or Mr. Gladstone, is encountered, but owners generally, if they give the matter any thought, are more concerned with finding something that slips easily off the tongue.

With the aristocrats it is otherwise. A glance down any list of prize-winners will reveal names beyond the dreams of most cat owners. How far removed are such names as Lavengro of Dunesk, Moonrise of Pensford and Trenton Raffles, which are common currency wherever champions meet, from the Tibbies and Gingers that knock the lids off dustbins and curdle the blood with midnight serenades. Misslefore Syrinxprint, with due respect, might have been taken from the pages of JAMES JOYCE, and Leinadsen Gardenia from the index to a seed catalogue. What, one wonders, happens when Sarisburg Sarissa or Fernreig Phraspeta has to be called in from the back garden ? The answer may be found among the aristocracy of canine society. This year's champion of champions at Cruft's, a graceful greyhound called Treetops Golden Falcon, is reported to be known within an intimate circle as "Goose." One can only assume that what applies to one applies to all, that Rothara the Smuggler of Penavon becomes in the privacy of his own home just Smuggler, that the imposing Whistonia Miss Prim of Meadowrock becomes plain Miss R., and that more manageable substitutes are found for such proud beauties as Rapscallion of Rhinevale, Sparrowswick Diamant Noir, and Thornfalcon Flipettywitch.

The ingenuity, and frequently the dignity and beauty, of titles among the elite of cats and dogs exceeds anything that the human race has evolved for itself. But among cats at least there is a marked falling-off lower down the social scale. Their names show a paucity of ideas rising sometimes as GLADSTONE said of the Irish speeches on Home Rule, to the level of mediocrity. Whether any of it matters very much to the cats may be doubted.

> Cruel, but composed and bland,
> Dumb, inscrutable and grand,

they carry their names lightly whether these be splendid, excruciating, or just dull. Nor does it matter very much from the point of view of their owners, for whatever we call them they hardly ever come.

ORWELL THAT ENDS WELL ?

BIG Brother is in a bad way. He has been taking punishment right and left these last few days. Not only has he just received something like a 600,000-word beating in Moscow—we now understand a phenomenon that has puzzled us for a long time : why the photographs of such supposedly dynamic people as the Communists invariably show human beings looking slightly dazed— but also the film world has decided that the time has come to cock a snook at him. They have determined that in Britain, at all events, he shall not be left having it all his own way at the end of *Nineteen Eighty-four*. Instead (after the mutual confession of betrayal) of the last bleak scene in the Chestnut Tree café with Winston finally overwhelmed by his love for Big Brother, affairs are henceforth to take an altogether more hopeful turn. Winston, we are told, will now from hundreds of British screens shout " Down with Big Brother ! " ; be shot ; find himself alongside Julia who is shot too ; and then——. And then, according to a writer in the *Daily Mail,* " lovingly their hands reach towards each other, and though they die with the autumn leaves swirling past them, the film sounds a note of undying hope." Lights up. Chocolates ? Cigarettes ? Ice cream ?

Here is a pretty kettle of cod fish. And here is a pretty exercise for the critics, the sociologists, and the philosophers. But admitting it's pretty, is it art ? The producer is represented as holding the view that at any rate it's logic. His ending, he is reported to have said, is more logical than ORWELL's. ("All men are logical, but some men are more logical than others " ?) Leaving this on one side, with a regret that ORWELL's shade cannot give us his sardonic observations on this latest exercise in Newspeak (and also on the statement that the new ending is the kind of thing ORWELL might have written if he had not known he was dying when he wrote the book), we are even more fascinated by the second aspect. Why is this piece of unpleasant nonsense (in the place of pleasant sense) reserved for British audiences only ? Are the British the only " logical " race ? Or can it be that the ridiculous hubbub there was over the B.B.C.'s most excellent piece of public service in televising *Nineteen Eighty-four* as ORWELL wrote it has so shattered national morale that the film world—those moguls with their fingers on the pulse of a public that always has its heart in the right place—are convinced it cannot take the truth twice ? As for the philosophers, they at least have something to replace the great " Kiss me, Hardy "—" Kismet, Hardy " debate as a study in national attitudes. Meanwhile, will no one besides MRS. ORWELL get angry with the film makers ? What kind of a people do they think we are ?

BANJO ON MY KNEE

BANJOS are, it appears, the rage in America and sales there are three times what they were last year. " And young Mr. Clayton, playing the banjo on his walking stick, sang ' Waiting for the Robert E. Lee ' "—thus KATHERINE MANSFIELD in a story set in the 1914 War, which, with the years immediately preceding it, seems to the backward-looking eye the golden age of the banjo. It was the chosen instrument of those groups of nigger minstrels which once turned the sands at the holiday season into places of enchantment for the young. Perhaps the songs and the jokes which went with the strumming lacked sophistication, and, if precisely reproduced now to compete with the high pressure forms of popular entertainment emanating from loud-speaker or television set, would seem as lost, as dated, and as faded as the photographs which show bathing machines standing up to the top of their wheels in water with weirdly garbed figures emerging from them. Yet to the ear of memory the notes of those banjos carry a most melodious twang.

MR. CHARLES RUBOVITZ, who is reopening a banjo factory in the United States, would not agree with all this. " Times are fast, loud and happy," he is reported as saying. " So is the banjo. That is why people want to hear its music." It is easy to see what MR. RUBOVITZ means. The banjo can, of course, be fast and loud. The guitar, one of its relations, going " Ting, Tong, Tang," worked up a magnificent pace and rhythm in BELLOC'S " Tarantella," and what a guitar can do, the banjo can make a shot at. Yet somehow for the banjo to be fast and loud seems to be a contradiction of its true nature, like occasional fits of boasting in a normally modest

106

man. The banjo is certainly a lively instrument, but it likes also sentimentally to express the vague nostalgia of the Southland ; it yearns to be back with mammy and the old folks at home ; it is at one with the feel and emotions of evening.

> When the mist was on the rice-fields an' the
> sun was droppin' slow,
> She'd git 'er little banjo an' she'd sing
> " Kulla-lo-lo ! "

Perhaps both KIPLING and MR. RUBOVITZ are right.

ABSENTEES ALL

LES absents ont toujours tort. The words of DESTOUCHES sound as true to-day as they did two centuries ago, for the word absentee has acquired, rather unreasonably, a meaning that is almost exclusively derogatory. It is refreshing, therefore, to hear someone standing up for the word, if not for the worst implications of it, as LORD ESHER has done in the House of Lords. He believes in absentees, and, while everybody might not follow him so far as to describe themselves as such, they would surely agree with him that absenteeism is deeply embedded in our national way of life. It does not always go by that name, because, whereas it is easy enough to sit in judgment on others by describing them as absentees, it is much harder to apply the term to ourselves. Yet most of us from time to time are guilty, for lack of a better word, of the failure to be present.

Foreigners sometimes attribute to us a predilection for sitting on committees.

> Lord Lilac thought it rather rotten
> That Shakespeare should be quite forgotten
> And therefore got on a Committee
> With several chaps out of the City.

That is what foreigners would expect him to do, but if they inquired further they might find behind the predilection a fairly strong current running against attendance at committee meetings. There is a good reason for this, just as there is for the proportionately small attendances at meetings of any kind, ratepayers, voters, or shareholders. The reason is, to put it bluntly, that some of those eligible to attend are better employed doing something else. Fortunately, absenteeism—it is no less—in, for

108

example, the parochial church council or in the meetings of the body that administers the local hockey club, is not catastrophic. It even has certain advantages. A committee meeting which no one is unable to attend and at which each member expresses his views whether he has anything useful to contribute or not, may sound democratic ; but a mere quorum would do the work quicker. Besides in most cases and starting with the House of Commons, there would be acute physical discomforts if everyone attended at once.

On the social level a little judicious absenteeism also has advantages. The dinners and other public functions which impose some kind of obligation to attend—how overwhelming many people would find them if they could not at times gracefully become absentees ! The well chosen expression, " Among those who accepted invitations . . .," embraces not only those who were present, not only those who broke their legs skiing and had to refuse at the last moment, or those who were genuinely prevented from attending by " urgent and unforeseen business " ; it covers also those who accepted in good heart but for whom as the day drew near it all became too much of a bore. The truth is that this kind of absenteeism helps the world go round. It is a form of human load-shedding when the pace of life becomes too fast. It is necessary, of course, to frown upon absenteeism that flouts the course of common duty, but it is as well, as LORD ESHER reminds us, to keep it distinct from that other absenteeism which despises sheep-like attendance and which establishes in all walks of life the freedom of the individual to stay away.

BOILING DOWN SCOTT

WITH what dreadful facility an inch of harmless or even respectful criticism may turn into an ell of blasphemy ! The most passionate admirer of WALTER SCOTT and of *Redgauntlet* may say that Alan Fairford's instructions from his solemn old father might well have been abbreviated. Or he may suggest that the relations between Normans and Saxons in the reign of RICHARD I amount almost to a bore, but that as soon as Gurth, in the woods with Wamba, calls down the curse of St. Withold on his unruly porkers, we are swept away into a forest of pure magic, but after that the descent is all too lazy. Lately in *The Scotsman,* of all journals in the world, somebody who is presumably a man and not a monster, who may even be of Scottish blood, but prudently veils his ancestry under initials, has committed himself to an almost incredible degree. He holds that much of SCOTT's dialogue is " unnaturally slow, verbose and tedious, overcrowded with archaic and obsolete dialectical words, necessitating much consultation of annotations and dictionaries." The answer surely is that of course it is and equally of course that it does not really matter. Would anyone reading Meg Merrilies's denunciation of Godfrey Bertram pause to look up in the dictionary the precise meaning of " reise," a word that even Scottish people do not always know ? Would he think that Edie Ochiltree was something too archaic, as the devouring tide is coming ever nearer to the foot of the cliffs, when he calls himself an " auld gaberlunzie " ? It is a word that a Saxon does not know for sure how to pronounce : that z is always puzzling, but heaven forbid that he should search some wretched appendix for a definition.

These may be no doubt altogether too frantic views. The gentleman of the initials who wrote the letter has far more practical ones. He thinks it would bring some shrewd publisher a handsome profit if he could condense the Waverley novels, while " retaining the essential Scott." The first and most obvious, perhaps too obvious, objection is one of pure conservatism in regard to an ancient institution. Dominie Sampson found words for it when the laird of Ellangowan proposed to expel the gypsies that had so long dwelt on his land. " Ne moveas Camerinan," he said, but as Mr. Bertram had no notion of his meaning the warning was vain. Another objection is to the hand that shall do this impious boiling down. Is there one skilful enough ? There was once published a boys' edition of *Ivanhoe*. The knights in the tournament had full scope, as was right and proper, but when it came to one of the most romantic scenes in the whole world, Locksley's splitting of the willow wand, all that the condenser said was that the archers then shot for a prize and Locksley won. If such things can be, it is better that every parent should learn the art of skipping, which is sometimes undeniably necessary for reading SCOTT ; but away with notes, which have made many a holiday task for ever hateful !

THE BOTTOM DRAWER

THERE is something of the collector in all of us. Although only the favoured few have a flair for picking up Georgian spoons on the cheap or lighting on old envelopes stamped with Penny Blacks in odd corners of the attic, the rest of us all have some haphazard hoard of belongings which, like jackdaws, we have amassed over the years. It is a little hard to give any reason for keeping a pile of old prep. school magazines, an incomplete pack of cards backed by a brewery advertisement, a French franc, the return half of a railway ticket from Windsor to London, and a bottle of violet ink. Even if such débris is worth nothing, we pretend that its sentimental value is incalculable. When we come to write our autobiographies — a moment that those who live to tell the story of their lives impatiently await—it will all be grist to the mill. Those school magazines will recall deeds of valour in the field which might otherwise have gone the way of other feats by mute, inglorious Huttons. Only the reader of the two-volume work will occasionally wish that the author had not preserved his records with such scholarly passion.

" You never know when they might come in handy," we say of a mint pair of male suspenders, a Christmas present from—which aunt was it? The trouble is, you never do know when they might come in handy. In fact, it is highly improbable that they will ever come in handy. Imagine yourself building houses of cards with your incomplete packs (it is hard to see how else to employ them), reading semi-literate and monstrously flattering reports of prep. school concerts, trying to force an outlandish disc of adulterated nickel into the reluctant slot of the gas meter, or announcing to your colleagues, with unconvincing bravado, that you have been completely converted to the virtues of violet ink (at least until the bottle runs out). Any such attempt to use the various bits of one's *impedimenta* (the howler " impediments " is right for once) must be proof of their uselessness. So a sensible man burns his boats and burns his bits and pieces. His purgative relish is a trifle marred by the feeling that he is saying good-bye to a bit of himself. Only when the last smoke of the pyre has cast its pall over the already ailing shrubs in his neighbour's garden is he hit by the thought that somewhere in the ashes lie the remains of his School Certificate. Bitterly does he rue his bout of spring cleaning. He is appalled by his rashness in tossing such a priceless possession into the flames. Not that he would ever have needed it, of course.

IN HOT WATER

IT is a curious thing that to get into hot water means figuratively to get into some extremely unpleasant predicament whereas in fact it is one of the pleasantest of all luxuries. Many people, whether they bathe in Jordan or in the rivers of Damascus, must have read an article on Bath with beautifully relaxed memories and heartfelt longings for their own particular waters of healing. It may be said that the joys of a hot bath can be obtained at home with less trouble and expense, but this is a shortsighted view. Anybody can feel lazy in hot water but laziness can prick the too active conscience, and so spoil some of the fun ; to feel virtuous too, to know that the more completely shameless the idleness, the greater the virtue, is to attain a poignancy which a mere domestic tub can never afford. There is, moreover, a solemn and formal parade, as it were of execution, which enhances the victim's sensations. He is led to his bath, robed in sacrifical garments, though perfectly capable of tottering there himself, and is gently and encouragingly submerged, as if he were a small boy putting a trembling foot into the waves on a first visit to the sea. Once safely in and left to himself he can play various and childish games, agitating the water with a toe so that it makes constantly changing patterns on the sunlit wall. He looks the while with grudging eyes on the sands in the hour glass which relentlessly proclaim that all things come to an end and that sooner or later he will have to get out. Discipline must now be maintained : the procession is reformed, more robes are put upon him, and he is escorted back to his cell for the agreeable ordeal of the hot pack.

This absolute surrender to rules is not without its charm, and the doctor, like that one who staked his

114

professional reputation on the fact that crumpets were not wholesome, is invariably " wery fierce." If he says the victim must lie on his bed after his bath there is no violent disinclination to obey him. This is indeed the real triumph, the very absolute of virtuous laziness. It is likely enough that he has always expressed a loud contempt for those who indulge regularly in a "rest." A little casual snooze in an armchair after lunch is one thing ; a deliberate and recumbent courting of repose is quite another. It is what some of his uncles used to do, and though he may now be nearly as old as they were once he has never yielded to such unmanly habits. And yet here he is now having to obey orders and finding the rest eminently soothing. He probably develops a conscience on the subject, but it is the reverse of that conscience that made him leap prematurely out of his bath at home. If he is aware of having lain down for less by five minutes than the time sternly prescribed, he shirks his doctor's eye and passes by on the other side, lest he get into hot water.

LOOKING FOR GRANDFATHER

SOME American service men, exiled on duty in this island, are amusing themselves by the good old game of Family Origins. Under whatever name you call it—Spot the Forebear, Who Was Great-Great-Grandfather? How Far Back Can We Go?—it is evidently great fun for those who like it. Most of us start more or less from scratch. We remember our grandparents, may have heard stories of their parents from our not certainly reliable aunts, and get lost in the sands of time after a pilgrimage of only a pitifully few generations. Those whose roots are in the Celtic fringes play this game with the most zest. The clan system is a powerful help. You can easily persuade yourself that you are directly descended from a hero on the losing side at Culloden, from one of the many kings of Ireland, or from a forager who went with OWEN GLENDOWER when the going was good across the Marches.

The confusing and unimaginative English system of surnames is unhelpful. But it is no barrier to determined detectives who are prepared to take the trouble to browse through the records at Somerset House and in country churches. For the sceptic, the unrewarding side of this hunt is that, in ninety-nine cases out of a hundred, the most that can be found is here a name and there the date of a marriage or a death. How tantalizing that those faded entries that the vicar is so patient in turning out for us do not include a candid report of what was said, off the record, at our great-great-great-grandfather's funeral by his surviving relatives. We might, if we could hear echoes of those far off *têtes-à-tête*, glow with filial pride. And we might not. Still, nothing is worse than ignorance, and it will have been noted that those who do have long knowledge of their family trees take as much pride in an uncle, several times removed, hanging on a capital charge from one of the branches as in a bishop or a battle-scarred commander.

One thing is certain. If each of us could be provided with an uncensored family dictionary of biography going back over the centuries, we should suffer some shocks. Such a reference work would prove invaluable to defending counsel if we ever found ourselves in the dock. How, he would ask, can a man whose direct ancestors got into such variegated scrapes be expected to keep straight? On balance it is, perhaps, best to rely on those learned agencies in America which (for a fee) will trace us back to WASHINGTON and (for an appropriately larger fee) to the Captain of the Mayflower. Failing that, we can all boast, with the proud character in *The Mikado,* that we are of pre-Adamite descent and go back to a protoplasmal, primordial, atomic globule. At any rate, nobody can contradict us.

TYPISTS ON THEIR TOES

A SUGGESTION, good as far as it goes, has been made by the French Secretaries' Association. The ladies who belong to this body cover, so it is calculated, seventeen miles a day on their fingers over the keyboard. This means—they claim—that their fingers make a journey equivalent to that from Paris to Washington in 240 days. No wonder, then, the Association argues, that the secretarial day is a hard one and that, to be made bearable, the burden of exercise should be spread over other parts of the body than the fingers. Then comes the suggestion. Secretaries who feel run down should try flitting round the office on tiptoes, letting the muscles play freely. It would be a pretty sight. But why should secretaries alone refresh themselves by a change of exercise?

Hard-worked toes must often grow tired at Sadler's Wells, and ballet dancers might move more gracefully on their points if, at intervals in the morning's practice, they relaxed at a desk and learnt touch typing. No less certainly, senior executives, whose non-stop dictating leads to that journey being made to Washington, might do themselves a power of good by touching their toes and performing hand presses on the floor of the office. Some of them admit to starting the day by deep breathing and other convolutions in the bathroom. Would they be too proud or too self-conscious to have a break for exercise with the ladies in business hours? The typists, flitting round on tiptoe, while the General Manager did cartwheels, would add alike to the gaiety of passing messengers and to the tautness of abdominal muscles in all concerned.

Once upon a time, old and young listened simultaneously to the persuasive instructors (and instructresses) of the B.B.C. and sat down to breakfast triumphantly aware that they had been up in the morning early, giving their sluggish bodies something to think about. A musical programme of exercises put on by the B.B.C. at, say, four in the afternoon would surely be better for productivity on the last lap of the working day than yet another cup of tea. But just as dietists find their pleas for eating less of that and more of the other fall on the deaf ears of objectors who maintain that a lot of what they fancy does them good, so the physical exercise fiends come up against a large unbelieving minority. It boasts that it never walks a yard when it can ride, has not done anything strenuous since it left school, is as fit as ever it was, and that its waistline compares favourably with that of its old contemporary, the rowing blue of yesteryear. SIR WINSTON CHURCHILL gave scandalous encouragement to these lazybones with his famous rebuke of the General who insisted on all ranks running seven miles a day. Could NAPOLEON have run seven miles across country at Austerlitz, he asked, answering his own question with " Perhaps it was the other fellow he made run." Perhaps there may even be some secretaries who will echo that sentiment.

FIVE POUND FOOLISH

TRADERS at Harwich have been told that five pound notes may be included in sailors' pay packets. The announcement should do much to remove the cloud under which this slightly bizarre piece of currency has long been languishing. A good many things lag behind the cost of living and there, clearly visible in the throng, is the one-time symbol of the spendthrift, flimsy, aloof, and maligned. In public esteem it has not advanced much since the twenties and thirties when its value, in terms of what it would buy, was considerable, and when there appeared to be something eccentric, to say the least of it, about the possession of one. In those days, as now, bus conductors, newsvendors, and the village shop quite reasonably recoiled at the sight of a " fiver," but even in large stores and restaurants its appearance led to the erection of a barrier of suspicion and to a general lowering of voices. So at least it seemed to the unfortunate owner as his name and address were politely taken and the number of the note jotted down, as though there were grounds for believing that he had spent the morning robbing a bank or manufacturing counterfeit in the basement of a disused villa.

Any attempt to hand the money over unostentatiously usually failed. The note, because of its size, had to be folded into the wallet, and since it carried no distinguishing marks on its back, it was necessary to unfold it again before parting with it in order to ensure that the owner was not surrendering a cleaners' ticket or the address of an old school friend of his wife's whom he had to entertain or call on. Even where the distinctive rustling of the paper and the spreading out of the note like a small table-cloth

120

could be avoided, there remained the danger that an over-zealous salesman would submit the owner to the indignity of holding the note up to the light before retiring with a puzzled frown to consult his superior. In time, of course, the transaction went through. The recipient put the best face on it he could, and after ransacking the till and his own pockets passed over with a wintry smile a quantity of change which would have been gratifying if the proceedings had not long since rendered the customer incapable of any such feeling.

Not everyone encountered so much trouble. Rich men of habit who only dined or shopped where " they were known," could shed a five pound note without difficulty, but the sense of doubt and inconvenience that it aroused generally brought it into disfavour. Something of that reluctance still exists, although the note has come within reach of a much wider public. It has not quite lost the unreasonable implication that where there is one note there are more, and that the gains they represent, if not ill-gotten, exceed the requirements of a moderate person. The fact that it has been found desirable to inform the traders of Harwich of their likely appearance is an illustration of this. No such feelings, however, will trouble the lower deck, and this breath of sea air may in time make itself felt farther inshore than Harwich.

SAY IT WITH IAMBICS

VERSE, whose waning popularity is so often lamented, has also been shorn of almost all its practical applications. It lingers on in a functional capacity in the excruciating quatrains which advertise some proprietary brands ; but its didactic status has declined to the level of the mottoes in Christmas crackers. When the DISTRICT JUDGE at Baden-Baden the other day ascended to rhyming couplets for the delivery of his judgment, the plaintiff who lost her case felt, understandably enough, that she had been cheated of the full solemnity of the law. Her appeal to a higher tribunal elicited the ruling that a judgment is no less valid because it happens to scan, and the Appeal Court, to reinforce its point, delivered its own judgment in rhyme. The plaintiff's feelings of outrage can have been no less than CROESUS'S would have been if in the opposite case, having staked the fortune of his armies on the oracular insight of the Pythian priestess, her answer had been returned in prose. So far have the Muses fallen.

No one nowadays would conceive, as VIRGIL did with his best seller, of committing his treatise on bee-keeping to verse. Even as a means of registering the virtues of the dead on their tombstones, where the pious custom is continued at all, verses are in eclipse. Verse teaches no one atomic theory as it did the ancient Greeks ; it records no epic battles of the twentieth century ; it sways no multitudes. It is true that SIR ALAN HERBERT, who has an agreeable way of breaking into rhyme on the most unlikely occasions, did once attempt to influence the House of Commons in its consideration of the Population

(Statistics) Bill by reading what he described as a " memorandum " in verse, LORD PAKENHAM, too, quoted a Treasury minute in verse in the Lords when moving the second reading of a Superannuation Bill ; the Bill was read a second time nonetheless. But in most places, including the Courts, the habit has fallen into desuetude.

Yet there are signs that some of our statesmen sometimes try to take tentative steps in the direction of poetic rehabilitation. SIR WINSTON CHURCHILL once countered the critics of diplomatic long windedness with the comment " Better to talk jaw to jaw than go to war." And the PRESIDENT OF THE UNITED STATES—or was it MR. BUTLER? —has made the useful discovery that " trade " rhymes with " aid." One day as their prosody improves they may wake up and discover, with the delighted surprise of M. JOURDAIN, that they have been talking all along in verse.

SPRING IN THE PARK

WHEN the spring sunshine awakens a man once more to a fresh awareness of his surroundings, and takes his mind back to other springs which first suggested to his infant mind that the earth was a beautiful place, it is not invariably a shining river that he remembers, or solitary hills, or green fields and greening woods. It may be, if he was a town mouse and nurtured among bricks and mortar, nothing more than a public park. A town park is a poor thing to set beside the country, but for many a man, before his legs grew strong enough and his spirit independent enough to carry him to the moors or the mountains, a park was his English heaven, air, rivers, " suns of home." It was here that he was pushed along in his perambulator, and here that he made his first close contacts with Mother Earth—though large areas of the Mother Earth in the place might have been carefully concealed by Father Macadam and his associates. The ratio of gravel and asphalt to grass and flowers and water was likely to be in the neighbourhood of two to five. And yet enough of Nature remained, enough at least to mark the passage of the seasons.

It is not necessarily the birds and the flowers that flash from time to time upon the inward eye of the man thus indebted to the park. The annual spring visit in a party from school, to draw the bursting buds in the botanical garden, is remembered less for its intrinsic excitement than for the relief it afforded from ordinary lessons. The annual furbishing of the boathouse and the tea chalet were much more satisfying signs of spring and of the return to a fuller life—the boathouse from which the Princess Ida would soon be setting sail round the little-more-than-a-duckpond with cargoes of small children gazing down into 18in. depths, the tea chalet that was the right trusty standby of mothers in the long summer holidays, when the children grew bored and tea in the park was a sure diversion. In school-time the park had other uses. It was the obvious place to play truant in and, though adults might wonder what a child could find to do there alone all day, truants were untroubled by such trifling problems.

At weekends in the summer in these present days there are concert parties in the park, and *A Midsummer Night's Dream*, and roller skating. The former patron will remember that in his young days it was always brass bands. Good brass bands, too, for the audience was expert. The best bands in the country were summoned to the park and the local paper sent its music critic. The children might be deaf to musical points, but they could not be blind to uniforms of scarlet. For the rest, it was their parents who enjoyed it most—the band and the sunshine and the gossip with friends ; their parents, and those older brothers and sisters who had reached the mysterious stage of washing without being told, and going for walks without father and mother, and flirting with the opposite sex. Though the last phenomenon, to be sure, did not wait on summer bands. It all began, in the park, in spring.

HOLIDAYS FOR HORSES

MIXED feelings may well be caused by the news that some working city horses are being given staggered holidays on a farm. As their stables are in the heart of town, and it is years since any of them had their shoes off and enjoyed a good roll on the grass, they richly deserve a break. A horse in a field, with nothing to do but eat and loaf or, if the spirit moves him —as it sometimes does even in the most elderly cases—to go tearing round, snorting happily as he goes, is a classic example of contentment. The only catch is boredom through having no company, and this will be avoided for these holiday makers because they are going in pairs. But one cannot help speculating on whether a precedent is being set. Other horses may have had leave before, but here are famous ones, who have drawn between them the coaches of MR. SPEAKER and the LORD MAYOR.

Is it not likely that their good fortune may lead to questions in a nation that only allows babies to win the popularity stakes against animals by a short head? Why should only a handful of privileged Shire horses be granted a right that is no longer withheld from any human worker? The apparent injustice cannot be ignored by comforting ourselves with GEORGE ELIOT's reflection that animals are such agreeable friends, because they ask no questions and they pass no criticism. No one who has been on friendly terms with any creature, four-footed or winged, will accept that proposition for one moment. Does the horse that has strolled up to the fence, with the idea of being fed out of a hand, pass any criticism if the owner of the hand has nothing to offer? He would be a singularly thick-skinned observer who answered that question in the negative.

126

Birds can move a vote of no-confidence as emphatically if crumbs and fat have run out as they can, and do, if their domestic nesting arrangements are disturbed.

Wild things must look after themselves so far as holidays are concerned and cats, in this context (and in a good many others) can be classed as wild. No cat would thank you for taking it away from home—not even to stay with a fishmonger whose shop was overrun with mice. But what about dogs? The case for packing them off on holidays is strong, both from their own point of view and that of their owners. You sometimes hear people say that holidays apart are a good family gambit. Absence makes the heart grow fonder on reunion. If this is true of human relations, surely it also applies to our dealings with dogs. Experience has proved, time and time again, that an " only " dog who is a quarrelsome little beast at home turns into a good mixer in kennels. The proposal for a regular, annual fortnight in which dogs lead a pack life and see as little as possible of human beings and nothing at all of their masters and mistresses is worth, at least, sending to the committee stage.

GHOSTS OF THE CELLAR

WHEN an old man or a man of middle life looks back to his early childhood and remembers his fear of the dark it may occur to him that the houses of other days really were more frightening places at night than the smaller houses of to-day. It lies so deep, that instinctive fear, in all of us, in brave men as well as little children, that it never will be eliminated until the millennium come ; but at least it is better understood now, and more wisely handled —and architects and builders have unwittingly helped the psychologists to bring comfort to fearful small hearts. What can there be to be afraid of in a small, neat, average modern home? Any little thing will do, of course, for childish fears to work upon, but most of what might be called the apparatus of bogydom has been swept away. He would be a pretty desperate, deluded boggart that decided to take refuge in the refrigerator or in one of the few small, much used cupboards of the modern household, a fortunate phantom who discovered a dark corner that was not regularly flooded with electric light—that superior magic with which so many demons have been exorcized. The little ones' fears may not be far away when bedtime comes, but neither is the light switch—and perhaps there is the wireless too, faint but friendly down below.

How different it was in the stately villas of yesteryear! Anything might be lurking up those dimly lighted stairs, on those long corridors with a tiny gas jet at the end of them (perhaps they were not so very long, but they seemed so then), behind those voluminous curtains, in the far recesses of those large cupboards, in the roomy sideboard or the harmonium, up in the attic or down in the cellar. Above all (or below all), down in the cellar. The attic

128

might be shunned at night, but it was a friendly playroom in the daytime, a great place for romping about, an inevitable refuge in all games of pursuit ; but the cellar offered no more than a chill, dim welcome on the sunniest days. Bolder spirits might use it in their games, might even venture there at night with candle or taper, in fearful expectation of they did not quite know what, but smaller, sensible little folk stayed carefully above ground, feeling more confident there.

In a practical sense there was much to be said for the cellar. " Keep in a cool place "—how easy it was to follow that injunction with a cellar at command. Is it mere imagination, or was the butter better that was kept on the stone shelves down there? Certainly the joints were larger that waited in the meat safe or under the meat cover. And if father kept a bottle or two in those cool, dark recesses he might truly refer to his " cellar " in another sense, which he could not do in these times when his wines are confined to a corner of the sideboard or a minute reserve in the larder. Cellars are outmoded now— missing altogether in the newer houses and abandoned to dust and decay in more and more of the older houses where they still exist. Not to regret them on some counts is impossible, but they made weary work for housewives and servants and to grow sentimental about them would be foolish. That may be left to the evicted ghosts.

K

B FOR MUTTON

NOWADAYS, when a voice over a Service line or
radio telephone makes the romantic-sounding statement, " November Tango Romeo," it means, unexcitingly
in fact, only N.T.R.—Nothing to Report. In the last war,
and until a short time ago, the voice (meaning the same
thing) would have said Nan Tare Roger, and before 1942
would have said Nuts Toc Robert. Thus, drastically,
have " they " changed yet again the Signals phonetic
alphabet designed to prevent confusion between letters
when named singly. This time, it is understood, it has
been with an eye, or rather, an ear, to the matter of the
comprehension of the many-tongued men of the forces of
the November Alpha Tango Oscar countries.

Certainly things to-day in this branch of Service verbal
communication are a lot less simple than the Ack Beer
Charlie of the signallers of the First World War, or even
the Able Baker Charlie of the Second, though, to be sure,
Charlie still goes on. It is still he who follows the Alpha
Bravo of the latest phonetic alphabets, and X-ray too
appears to be as steady and constant as might be expected
while Victor, who once was " matily " just Vic, at least
is staying as he was during the last war. But it is disturbing
to see that William has taken to Whisky, and sad that
Peter, the pleasant though on the whole less effective
successor to the strong, unmistakable Pip of long ago,
now gives place to a most feeble Papa. Time-honoured
Sugar is somewhat inadequately succeeded by Sierra, and
good old George, after all these years, is going in for Golf.

Yet there is one Army Signals unit, once of yeomanry,
now of parachutists, who doubtless will stick to using,
among themselves, their own peculiar phonetic alphabet

evolved in the Western Desert by the squadron which served with the 22nd Armoured Brigade. This began bluntly with A for 'Orses (hay for horses), B for Mutton (beef or mutton), C for Thighlanders (Seaforth Highlanders), and went on in an ascending scale of the higher lunacy to verbal atrocities like M for Sis (emphasis), R for Askey (Arthur Askey), and X for Breakfast (eggs for breakfast). But even by those unorthodox practitioners the receipt of a message was strictly acknowledged, as messages still are acknowledged (in spite of Romeo), by the regulation formula, Roger (meaning R or " received ")—Out!

WIGGLES TO THE RESCUE

IT is an uncomfortable paradox that whereas to faint has always been considered effeminate in men, it is generally the soldier who is seen by so many to fall a victim to it. Students in operating theatres and schoolgirls in chapel may collapse in greater numbers but it is the ceremonial soldier who creates the greater stir. The army has not hitherto been able to do very much about it, for it is caught, so to speak, in the web of its own efficiency. A sergeant-major throwing buckets of water over swaying units of personnel would disrupt the splendour of any parade, and what a travesty would be made of military precision and bearing if Trooper Bloggins, on recognizing in himself the first symptoms of Consciousness (Loss of), were empowered to ground arms, to remove headgear, and to stick his head between his legs. Even the administering of sal volatile becomes difficult in an assemblage which depends for its success on stillness and coordination of movement.

It matters little that a fair sprinkling of those who come to watch are themselves borne away on stretchers before the fun is finished. It matters even less that if the public were subjected to the same test it would go down like nine-pins. A member of one of the bravest units in the British Army with a list of battle honours as long as his arm has gone off into an old-fashioned swoon. The rifle clatters to the ground, the crowd gasps, the cameras, whether they want to or not, have recorded the ignominy. The battalion does the only possible thing : it pretends nothing has happened, and carries on, splendidly indifferent to its fallen comrade. Nevertheless the blight remains, and commanding officers were no doubt glad to learn that

132

medical research has at last turned its attention to the matter. A cure, or more accurately, a preventive for fainting on parade has been devised that is both simple and, more important, invisible to the critical eye of the spectator. The announcement is couched in appropriate language. The intention is " to prevent venous pooling of the blood and abnormal filtration of the fluid of blood into the leg tissues," but the action to be taken is unmistakable. It is, put simply, to wiggle the calf muscles.

What would our great-grandmothers have made of all this? They were not ashamed to faint themselves. The fug and tight-fitting clothes sometimes made it spontaneous, and no one would suggest that, when, for example, Lady Clara gave a little shriek and fell lifeless on the gravel-walk at the sight of the hairy-faced Jack Belsize, she was acting a part. For all that, her generation knew how to use fainting as an instrument of policy or as a mental safety-valve. An easy, self-applied cure would not have suited their book. The soldier has no need for such reservations. When he faints he is not enlisting the sympathy of others. He is, officially at least, more likely to be regarded as a culprit than a casualty. If wiggling the calves can do the trick, it will save embarrassment all round, not least among the public.

FLAG DRILL

NOBODY envies those whose lot it is to raise money for charity. The cause is sure to be deserving but the difficulty is to arouse in other people the same conviction, and the rebuffs that are inseparable from the work are unlikely to be reduced by the weight of taxation and by the ministrations of the welfare state. That these rebuffs have not materially increased is suggested by the figure for Remembrance Day collections. Given that the cause is of first importance and has a nation-wide appeal, it is still remarkable that a sum not far short of a million pounds should have been counted as the harvest of the poppy.

Not all of it will have been taken in the collector's box, and yet those who carry the little trays right into the enemy's camp, as it were, account for a large number of victims ; nobody could feel much resentment at being held to ransom in a good cause, and if he did he would still be free to exercise his independence. The general feeling about flag selling is rather more complex. The victim pays up without flinching, the more so when the cardboard emblem is pinned to his lapel with a smile. He is a cheerful giver all right, but there is a slight feeling of self-reproach that he is not also a spontaneous one. It is sometimes all too apparent that he was cornered and that, short of crude evasion, there was no escape. He may, of course, try to prevent what he cannot cure, but disguised evasive action is unlikely to succeed for long. A certain amount of tacking and staring into shop windows will get the miser or the conscientious objector to the end of the street, but well organized vendors know how to defeat such manoeuvres. Sooner or later, just as the malingerer is about to buy a paper or is emerging from his favourite restaurant or from a taxi, one of those trays steps out of the shadows and a pair of appealing eyes roots him to the spot. Excuses will avail him little. No one is in all that much of a hurry ; to protest that he has no change is to run the risk of being talked into giving more than he can afford ; while to explain that he has a private list of charities to which he confines himself must be deemed a rather pompous way of saving sixpence.

From these arguments two precepts suggest themselves. One, for the sellers, is that a happy mean between complete self-effacement and importunate interception best recommends itself to the buyers. Some born beggars will charm a pound note from the wallet of a mere acquaintance while they are going up in the lift, but it is a risky line of attack for the inexperienced. The other is that the buyer, for his part, might do worse than make up his mind that unless he can maintain an unswerving refusal he had better part with his money to the first box that he hears being rattled. In this way minor irritations may be avoided and the painless milking of the public's purse, even by the million, will go smoothly on.

MICE ON THE MARCH

MOST of us know from A. E. HOUSMAN (whether he was quoting, or adapting, or inventing makes no matter) that

> Clunton and Clunbury,
> Clungunford and Clun,
> Are the quietest places
> Under the sun.

Now from New South Wales come " Tottenham, Trundle, Tullamore, and Fifield," matching the famous Shropshire villages in euphony of rhythm. In euphony, perhaps—but not in their condition. This (according to Reuter, to whom is due this tripping addition to the poetry of place names) is at present far from quiet, for they are grievously disturbed with vast quantities of mice. These wee, sleekit, and hitherto no doubt cowering and timorous, beasties have been driven by a wet season from the fields they usually inhabit, and have invaded the four melodious towns, causing as much worry as ever did the rats in Hamelin. Indeed, the two cases seem in some ways oddly similar, for in Hamelin, it will be remembered, the rats " bit the babies in the cradles," while in Tottenham, Trundle, Tullamore, and Fifield " mothers are erecting mosquito nets around their children's beds at night to protect them from the mice."

No doubt it is all extremely unpleasant, and no doubt the citizens of T.T.T. and F. are entitled to everyone's sympathy. Yet it is just at this point that the reader begins to waver, and finds himself wondering whether it must not be a very feeble and pusilanimous mouse which allows itself to be daunted by a net intended to keep out a mere mosquito. To stir the tragic emotions

136

a certain grandeur of scale is necessary, and that the mouse
—particularly this mouse—most notably lacks.   The
point, it may be added, is not a new one.   We have
BOSWELL'S word for it that the poet JAMES GRAINGER,
when writing his epic *The Sugar Cane* originally began
a paragraph

> Now, Muse, let's sing of mice !

But, on reflection, made the passage " more dignified "
by altering it to

> Now, Muse, let's sing of rats !

The fact is that the mouse is a pretty little creature,
and much as we may dislike seeing too much of him at
too close quarters, we cannot (at least from a comfortable
distance) get very much worked up about him.   There is
a sort of notional cosiness and friendliness about mice
and even women (whose traditional abhorrence of the
species has for generations been one of the professional
humorist's most valuable properties) have been lured by
MR. WALT DISNEY into a certain kindly tolerance of them.
Who, having heard Mickey Mouse singing "I can't give you
anything but love, Baby," to his own piano accompaniment
and the delectation of Minnie Mouse, could again buy
a mouse trap, or look without slight compunction upon
even the most favourite of household cats ?   One may,
indeed, wish the good people of Tottenham, Trundle,
Tullamore, and Fifield well rid of their mice—and yet
doubt whether any Pied Piper will be moved to emigrate
to New South Wales to offer them his help.

MIND MY EGGS

SHADES of the old squire and of his man-trap, now only to be seen in museums ; an angry gamekeeper in Versailles is in trouble with the police for having peppered a French Air Force helicopter with gunshot. The din of its engine, he protests, was ruffling the domestic calm of his pheasants. " The slightest noise," he is reported as having said, " might ruin my entire crop of eggs." Happily for the crew, the wrath of the gamekeeper made him fall below his normal level of marksmanship. He failed to score a direct hit. The human targets, on a training flight for Algerian operations, were unhurt and the helicopter flew back, as many a lucky pheasant has done, safely to its base. But the magnificence of the gesture remains untarnished. Gamekeepers, or such of them as there are left in this country, fight a losing battle against poachers with fast cars, magpies, and other vermin. How many of them still keep up the high spirits of their French colleague and are prepared to let fly at the biggest game ?

From their point of view and looking comfortably ahead, the helicopter casts beyond doubt a future shadow broader and darker than that of any winged thing. Compared with its possibilities of disturbing the peace and the countryside, those of jets are small beer. Already, we are told, wild life, that takes these matters much more calmly than men do, is beginning to adjust itself to the frightening challenge of the jet. Creatures that, a year or so ago, fled panic-stricken for safety, now take no more notice of the last word in screeches than cattle, browsing in meadows beside an arterial road, take of the cars hooting their way to a seaside lunch on a fine Sunday morning.

Helicopters will be less easy to ignore. They are the Paul Prys of the heavens. When they become as common,

138

as probably they will, as the family fourseater, they will hover over coverts, poise above the green turf of the Downs, now inaccessible to wheeled traffic, and sink down to picnic wherever their owners choose. This will be great fun for the owners, who will be a vast majority of the population. But it will be a sad day for game-keepers, if any of the species, persisting like mastodons, are still there to worry about their pheasants. The process may take long. A garage for aircraft in every self-respecting, semi-detached home may seem a far-fetched dream of the future. But so did the present state of affairs, fifty years off, when the automobile went abroad on the dusty roads heralded by a warning red flag. Those of us who enjoy the comedy of progress may well survive to read, on our excursions into the shires, the vainly menacing notice, " Helicopters will be prosecuted."

THE ONLY HOPE

IN some ways it is an idyllic scene. The family car, in the depths of which a matriarch, or anyhow a crone of some kind, is reading the Sunday newspaper, has been driven into the centre of the glade, leaving its orderly track upon the asymmetrical carpet of bluebells. The family have got a cheerful bonfire going just upwind of the young plantation, from the depths of which comes the ecstatic yapping of their little dog. Ample justice, judging by the detritus, has been done to the midday meal, and two of the children, in friendly rivalry, are throwing stones at some empty bottles. A portable wireless set fills the glade with melody.

The owner of the glade, flint-hearted, views this pastoral tableau with gloom. He knows all too well that picnickers, once they have infiltrated to some secluded spot, tend to return there on subsequent weekends, often bringing with them a carload or two of their friends, until in the end the public have established a right of litterage (if there is such a legal term) and the spot is secluded no longer. Now is the time to strike, before the invaders have consolidated their bridgehead. But what tactics is he going to use ?

The great thing, he knows from experience, is to avoid getting involved in an argument. It is, for instance, absolutely no good asking them how they would like it if he came and picnicked in their garden ; if he tries this gambit, it is Lombard Street to a china orange that they will turn out to be flat-dwellers. It is still more fatal to criticize them, or seem to criticize them, in any way— by, for instance, suggesting that they ought to keep their dog under control or discourage their children from

140

covering his property with broken glass. To mention pheasant's nests is dangerous in the extreme, for even if his visitors are not fanatically opposed to bloodsports he will put himself ideologically in the wrong by betraying an interest in the chase. And whatever approach he adopts there is always the risk that it will be countered by the demand to be told what harm they are doing anyhow.

This is a difficult question to answer. They have not yet set his woodlands on fire; he cannot prove that their beastly dog has blighted the prospects of a single brood of game. It is not much good pointing out that their Watteau-type arrangements have destroyed a number of beech seedlings, for there is no reason why they should believe his improbable assertion that these minuscule growths would have become large, beautiful and valuable trees in less than 150 years' time. He might perhaps shift them with a warning that the place abounds in snakes; but probably in the end he will take the usual course. Apologetic, ingratiating, like a suppliant craving some unreasonable boon, he will ask his visitors if they would very much mind, after they have finished their picnic, going away. " You see," he will say, in the shamed, deprecating voice of one pleading guilty to a grave charge, " this happens to be—well, er, as a matter of fact it's private property." They may go, or they may not; but on these occasions soft soap is the brutal landowner's only hope.

A POVERTY OF POETS

LAST year eighty-eight competitors entered for Suffolk's annual poetry prize in honour of GEORGE CRABBE, that resolute debunker of the rural scene ; this year there are only five. Such a slump as this defies ready explanation. Mild fluctuations in the Suffolk poetry market are to be expected ; a poet here, suffering from a rush of words to the head, hastening to join the ranks, a poet there, stricken with temporary dumbness, falling out ; but this wholesale desertion in the face of competition is something altogether different. It is as though a plague had stalked through the Suffolk lanes blighting the poetic fancies of the inhabitants, or, more prosaically, that by some freakish behaviour of the law of averages, as though all the members of a cricket eleven should choose the same match in which to score ducks, all the possibles found themselves out of form and determined to scratch at this one particular time.

There is, of course, something in the name and nature of a poetry competition, implying, as it does, writing to order, calculated to convince the Muse that she has urgent business elsewhere. Some Poet Laureates have, it is true, delivered the goods in the form of appropriate verses for special occasions with promptitude and aplomb, but less gifted mortals are inclined to feel themselves up against invisible obstacles. That inspiration of which A. E. HOUSMAN wrote, a physical thing making its presence felt in the pit of the stomach, in the lifting of the hairs on the face, is not a slave at the beck and call of the order to write clearly on one side of the paper and to post not later than such-and-such a date. The poet's eye, contemplating the situation, is less likely to roll in a fine

142

frenzy than to take on the glazed look of a codfish on a fishmonger's slab.

Whether the poems have to be written on the subject, as well as in the honour, of CRABBE is not clear from the *communiqué* announcing the disastrous casualties, but, if they have, the fall from eighty-eight to five becomes a shade more understandable. If Suffolk has an artistic hero, it is CONSTABLE, the painter, rather than CRABBE, the poet ; the flat eastern countryside does not boast a school of poets as do the lakes and mountains, and CRABBE has not the obvious appeal of the northern singers. "Alas, I've only been able to manage one line," confessed one of SIR COMPTON MACKENZIE's endearing comic characters. " It's a very good line as far as it goes, but it doesn't go nearly far enough," and so may have said many of the frustrated Suffolk hopefuls. But there is no need to despair. The writing of poetry is a tricky and unpredictable thing. The epidemic of scratching may have worked itself out and next year the entry may soar to the dizzy heights of three figures.

ANY OLD PIERS ?

THE ignominious end to which things come, CAESAR'S and ALEXANDER'S dust acting as stoppers of holes and the august journal of yesterday lighting to-day's fire, or, even yet more humiliating fate, wrapping fish-and-chips, is something to be borne philosophically, but, even so, it is difficult not to feel a pang of sympathy with, and regret for, the old pier at Sheerness which faces an uncertain future and has not, so far, found a buyer in the second-hand market. Piers, it is true, are not to-day what once they were, but then, like so many other things, they never were. The pier, however thronged it may be with adults and however grand the orchestra performing in the pavilion at the top, or in one of those half-way houses of which some piers boast, is something that belongs to childhood. Surely there are bathing machines flanking it on either side, but clearer in the memory than those shadowy and fantastic shapes are the click of the turnstile, mechanical gateway to paradise, and, thrilling and unforgettable, the hollow, important sound of one's own footsteps on the boards.

That a pier, any pier, should be threatened in June is ironic insult tacked on to potential physical injury, for, as with the lotus-eaters it is always afternoon, so with piers it is always summer. Pierrots have, of course, in derivation nothing to do with piers, but by assonance and association of ideas they have. That white, ample and vaguely Turkish dress, set off with black pompoms, is redolent of blue skies and the sun, and, although it was the concert party rather than the pierrot troupe that usually performed on piers—the pierrots preferring a stretch of sand near the entrance—yet they are a part of the general

144

look, feeling, and atmosphere of pierdom. Even more delectable to those small boys whose heroes were COLIN BLYTHE and K. L. HUTCHINGS were the slot-machines with figures of a batsman bearded in the image of THE DOCTOR. For a penny it was possible—perhaps it still is ?—to set in motion a lob bowler, a kind of D. L. A. JEPHSON, as it were, and the fate of the coin depended on whether the cunning underarm delivery would beat the DOCTOR's bat or whether he would drive it majestically into a hole marked " boundary."

When it did rain—as rain it must have done even in those enchanted days—piers could be faintly sinister places. Their air of forlornness and desertion would become exaggerated and the noise made by the sea slapping about among the pillars weird and menacing.

And now I'm here, from this here pier it is my fixed intent
To jump, as Mr. Levi did from off the Monu-ment—

But that was only BARHAM's fun. Piers have fundamentally happy natures, and may the promenade relations of the doomed specimen at Sheerness be ever spared a similar fate.

DEVON DUMPLINGS

WEST country school girls, if one of their medical officers of health is not maligning them, are in danger of getting a lean and hungry look. He is surprised to find " a comparatively poor take-up of milk " in the secondary schools attended by these young ladies and he darkly hints that this may be " attributed to adolescent concern about their figures." If the milk shy adolescents took courage from the posters they would lap up the healthy stuff by the pint. A film star in all her glamour could not look more photogenic than do the smiling blondes who, as the artists have painted them over the years, evidently do everything short of bathing in milk, and for whom a cocktail, with the most modest alcoholic content, would, no doubt, be a snare and a delusion. But there are sceptics in America no less than in our own far west, as may be deduced from the report that transatlantic teen-agers are tempted by skim milk offered encouragingly as slim milk.

The virtues of milk as a basic tipple are beyond question —as is the fear of growing fat. It is idle for the character in *Iolanthe* to have no objection to stoutness—in moderation. All of us, whether we are hoping to get into the hockey eleven next autumn or thinking that it is about time we cut down our golf, would prefer to line up with the fairies in *Iolanthe* than to be burdened with however modest a spread. Even great men have not escaped being laughed at for failure to control this particularly insidious form of inflation. The eagle eye of the lyricist noted (so far as memory can recall his words) that NAPOLEON grew too fat ; we all know that from pictures in the galleries ; he never really learnt the knack of laying off the calories.

Fat as butter, fat as a porpoise—the ominous old phrases will recur. Against them a mother of a school girl may recall to her comfort the reflection that a once famous beauty was toasted as fair, fat, and forty. But that would not go down at school, even if it were quoted on Speech Day by the most jolly and genial of medical officers of health. It would be equally futile—and ungallant into the bargain—to cite the leading cases of swimmers and singers of renown who have worn their ample stones with easy grace. The verdict of the fifth form will be in favour of those pale thin ones who, as handled by their Press officers, appear to be the life of Hollywood revels. No, the best hope for milk is to stand, as a nice drink, on its own merits, which, happily for the health of the rising generation, are as well known to many little girls as they are (with some interesting exceptions) to all kittens.

TWENTY THOUSAND LEAGUES
UNDER

THE Austrian diver whose marriage is reported to have been arranged to take place under water is going too far for most of us. He and his bride are to be married in diving dresses, which seems a damp and depressing way of embarking on wedded life. The minister, or registrar, the best man, the bridesmaids, and the guests will presumably have, for practical reasons, to be similarly clad. It will not be easy for the ushers in the circumstances to sort out the guests of the bride and the guests of the bridegroom and to arrange the aquatic congregation neatly in two ranks on the bottom. But this bizarre affair is a reminder of how, in a matter of only a few years, we have grown accustomed to the idea of being at ease below the surface.

Not so long ago the diver was an exotic figure, to be envied but not followed, except by the adventurous, as he disappeared trusting to that precarious pipeline. The only thing that would have induced most of us to put on his clumsy-looking armour would have been had the only alternative offered involved us in clasping a stone to our bosom and hurtling down with the pearl divers. Now, all sorts of strange new gadgets have made it possible even for amateurs, to do a little exploring, to look the fishes in the face and to admire the view of submarine gardens. So far, the depths to be reached by the most professional are still negligible in comparison with the more than Everest depth of the ocean. When optimists unhampered by any scientific knowledge, look forward to a coming day in which they will be able to stroll along the bed of the Pacific, they are put off by awkward facts about pressure. But the ignorant have long since ceased to take the caution of the scientists too seriously.

Who knows for certain that we shall not indulge in oceanic hiking before the first space ships come back on their homeward voyage and tell us what it is like on the neighbouring planets ? If so, many of us will be pleased. Would it not be more exciting to explore ancient wrecks and meet, perhaps, the sea-serpent or, at any rate, creatures as strange as he than to tramp over the bleak pastures of the moon ? What is more, there is something impudent about the Sphinx-like ease with which the oceans withhold their secrets from us. After all, they are part of this earth, and, in our efforts to get at them we cut figures no more dignified than those of small boys letting glass jars down into ponds. Let our daughters unto the last generation that ever is be married in church. But why should they not honeymoon in the Mindanao Deep ?

GIFT FISHES

WHILE a fisherman was fishing in the River Clwyd, Ruthin, a salmon leaped from the river into the lap of the angler, thus presenting him with the pretty problem of deciding whether to be pleased or annoyed. From the material point of view, there are, of course, no two questions about it. The basic aim of fishing is, or in the days of one's primitive ancestors was, to catch something to eat, and here is a choice and luscious delicacy provided free of all trouble and no questions asked. It would doubtless be ill-mannered and ungrateful to look so unexpected a gift fish from the river god in the mouth, but nevertheless the fisherman may be forgiven if he could not altogether suppress a spasm of irritation. No doubt the river god meant well, but gods, when they meddle in the affairs of mortals, sometimes make a mess of things, and those at the receiving end of their benevolent attentions are apt to mistake them for a fussy and unwarrantable interference.

Indeed there are few things harder to forgive than unsolicited help, especially when the task involved calls, as the practitioner would like to think, for an uncommon degree of craft and patience. Who knows what high ambitions the angler cherished as he started off, what deep strategic plans he had worked out, choosing the place for his operations with a shrewd, knowledgeable eye for cloud, wind, and signs of promise in the look of the water. Then the momentous decision as to the type of fly. Another fisherman less versed in the subtleties of the sport would, he cannot help thinking complacently to himself, plump for a striking little affair in orange and black, but he, with greater cunning and vision, decorates his rod with a more sober specimen, neat but not gaudy.

Even the non-fisherman, the far from compleat angler, can understand the fascination of the preliminary work and is capable of appreciating the skill that goes to the making of a perfect cast. Looked at in this light, the abrupt leap of salmon into lap does indeed seem a disconcerting occurrence, evidence of an over-officious desire to be of service, a wind—or, rather, a river—fall as unwelcome as unexpected. Humpty-Dumpty complained that it was provoking when people could not distinguish between a belt and a cravat ; fishermen must experience the same kind of emotion when salmon, disregarding all decent etiquette, jump enthusiastically to meet their doom instead of waiting for it to come to them in the seemly and proper way by means of rod and line. It is a tall story although the fish did not get away, but somehow it is not in the best fishing story tradition and would probably be met with cold disapproving silence in the bar parlour of " The Angler's Arms."

PUTTING OFF TILL TO-MORROW

DRAKE, who resolutely finished his game of bowls when the Armada was reported in sight, and KING CHARLES I, who played out his round of golf on the links of Leith when the news came to him of the Irish rebellion, have now two modern imitators of great distinction. MARSHAL TITO and MR. KHRUSHCHEV were recently to have signed a statement on the result of their conversations, but they put off this ceremony and remained in the Stadium to watch football. It is only right to add that as to CHARLES I there is another tradition that he instantly threw down his clubs and abandoned the game, and ANDREW LANG has proposed the disloyal theory that in that case his Majesty may have been four down with six to play. At any rate there is no such unworthy suggestion as to MARSHAL TITO and MR. KHRUSHCHEV. They doubtless said, in effect, " Football first, politics afterwards " and determined to see the end of the match. Everybody will sympathize with them. If DOCTOR JOHNSON had been alive he might have adapted a famous dictum of his and said that there are few ways in which a man can be more innocently employed than in watching football. The statement as to their conversations would have been just the same and just as important if it were signed a day later, but if they had left the Stadium five minutes before that flashing goal scored by the Dynamo centre forward had decided the issue of the day they might not have forgiven themselves for missing a supreme moment that could never be recaptured.

In order to enjoy that game they had to flout the vulgar prejudice in favour of not putting off till to-morrow what can be done to-day. This is a rather priggish maxim, popular with those who have already completed their income tax returns, been to see their new next-door neighbour in the village, written that letter to Aunt Belinda or performed other such tiresome duties. There is, we may hope, some merciful graduation in the postponement. In the bad old days of paying calls the young man who had deliberately arranged himself in the garb of sacrifice, had reached the fatal front door, and then rushed past it in sudden panic, felt himself for the rest of the day so feeble a creature that he enjoyed no comfort from the reprieve. If on the other hand he had said from the first that it was a fine afternoon and he was hanged if he was going to waste it in paying calls, he could still hold up his head. He felt as he had done a few years before when he heard the feet of those scampering into early school and simply rolled over in bed deserving the inevitable Georgic cheaply earned. He might be a fool but he was neither a whimperer nor a coward. In these days of Lord's and Wimbledon there will be many to imitate those two great figures at Moscow. Having declared that they will be back at the office at four precisely they will stay on and on, while the shadows lengthen on the grass, to see one more over or one more game. They will have followed an august example and the office will do very well without them.

OUT OF DOORS

"**B**UT stay!" bellows the tall man in the black and mauve doublet. "Who comes yonder?" His fellow-conspirator, in plum-coloured velvet, starts violently. "It is the Yuke!" he roars. He had meant to say "It is the Duke!" but a sudden squall of wind blew his starboard mustachio into his mouth and for a moment consonants were beyond him. Dexterously removing it, he shouts "Come, we'll conceal ourselves in yonder thicket." They sidle away and stand behind a small shrub, downstage left. "I wish those two men would go away," says a little girl at the extreme end of the front row. "I can't see anything now." "Hush, darling," says her mother.

The Duke, at the head of considerable retinue, is meanwhile making what is known in military circles as the advance to contact. He appears from his expressive gesture to be delivering a speech as he picks his way from a distance through the rank grass of the deer park (on such an inclement evening, the possibility that he is swatting midges scarcely exists); but the immortal words are carried away by the wind, which is violently agitating the branches of the trees above the actors' heads. In one of these trees, however, there must be a microphone concealed, for suddenly the audience is startled out of its misery by a stentorian but disembodied voice:

". . . the Earl of Pontefract, that wicked man,
By cruel curtailment of my uncle's dues—

Look here, George, it's no good my saying all this stuff now. They can't possibly hear a word. I'll start the speech again when we get there."

154

But this last-minute change of plan leads to complications. For the Fool is due to make his entrance from (as it were) deep long leg as soon as the Duke fetches up in the centre of the stage ; and since nobody is in wireless touch with the Fool he duly discards his duffle coat in the distant laurels, breaks covert, and comes capering over the soggy greensward with loud cries of " Hola, piggotty ! " " Wher's thy wanion, nuncle ? " and other witty remarks. This intrusion detracts from the pathos of the Duke's long account of his abominable treatment by the Earl of Pontefract, and for some time the players are at cross-purposes, Ulcerio, the good old courtier, being intent on delivering a speech beginning

> A tale so fiendish-vile I ne'er did hear,
> Save once, at Hounslow, in your father's time

and the Fool on singing an obscurely indelicate song about minnows.

But things sort themselves out after a bit. The Duke and his *cortège* shamble off in the gathering dusk, the man in the black and mauve doublet has a quarrel with the man in plum-coloured velvet, a young lady appears and most injudiciously lies down on the wet ground and pretends to fall asleep, a lot of sneezing fairies do a dance, and the Fool sprains his wrist turning a cartwheel. Amateur productions of SHAKESPEARE out of doors are not one of those facets of our national life with which the British Travel Association attempts to lure foreign tourists to our shores, nor are they among the highest expressions of our culture. But they are, if one stops to think about them, really rather extraordinary phenomena.

THE MASCOT PLAYS THE GOAT

WITHOUT going into deep anthropological origins or inquiring, with a side-glance at the scape-goat, why goats should so often serve as regimental mascots, it may be proclaimed without fear of contradiction that mascots, whatever their form and nature, are meant to bring luck. What happens, then, when the mascot itself is unlucky and, as with poor Billy, the goat-mascot of the 2nd Battalion, The Royal Welch Fusiliers, has ill-luck crossed with indignity ? Billy, who has left Singapore for treatment in England, broke a hind leg when he fell into a drain, and the omens which could be read from this particular occurrence are dreadful to contemplate.

The safest of mascots, from the point of view of the superstitious, must surely be the inanimate, the rabbit's foot, the charm, the " lucky " coin, which would somehow manage to preserve in the eyes of its besotted owner all its magical properties even if it should lose half a dozen tosses in succession. The worst that can happen to these is that they should get lost, and, while this may seem a disaster, it is not one so dire in prophecy as disaster occurring to a mascot endowed with a life of its own. When small boys arrayed in club colours accompany football teams on to the pitch before a cup-tie kick-off, those teams must have their hearts in their mouths lest the infant should trip and fall sprawling, while the kicking of the ball by a miniature boot into an empty net must seem as good as a ticket to Wembley. The animate mascot must indeed be a perpetual source of anxiety and its behaviour sometimes make the reading of the signs as difficult as the unravelling of the more complacently ambiguous utterances of the Delphic Oracle.

It is difficult for those who dislike goats to discuss them —the knowing, supercilious face finished off with a beard reminiscent of cartoons of Uncle Sam is so repugnant that any assessment of their value as mascots is impossible—but the regiment adopting one should know what to expect. But what if a regiment should be so foolhardy as to choose a cat ? Witches, it is true, have shown a distinct partiality for them as familiars, but what would suit a witch about to take off on a broomstick would hardly do for a regiment prepared to march past. The cat would certainly show an indifference to the proceedings which might damp enthusiasm, but at least it would not conjure up visions of catastrophe and humiliation by making such a fool of itself as to fall down a drain and break a leg. Still, human nature being what it is, and mascots being what they are, the recovery of Billy is certain to be the constant prayer and hope of the gallant Welshmen.

157

NOT WIMBLEDON

EACH year as Wimbledon comes round it proves again its power to stir up something more than the excitements of the day. It sets old buffers off, and middle-aged ones too, in pursuit of memories of the game, just as the mere mention of Lord's does in another context. More than Lord's does, indeed, in some quarters—though it be heresy to say so—for Wimbledon has a meaning in many a heathen land where they do not play cricket. So the veterans tell their tales of the DOHERTY brothers, who never rolled their sleeves up, and those who are not so veteran as all that remember SUZANNE LENGLEN, and the HELENS, and the "FOUR MUSKETEERS" of France, and TILDEN's confident mastery, and perhaps MISS TAPSCOTT from South Africa, that brave pioneer who played in the championships without stockings, in 1929.

It is not necessarily of Wimbledon, however, that some men reminisce at Wimbledon time. They may never have been there, and certainly they never dreamed, in their wildest dreams in their hardest-hitting days, of playing there. It is not the All England Club they remember but the half-grass, half-plantain courts of a little known club in a less famous suburb. It was a limb of the parish church, perhaps, or had grown out of and eventually swallowed the local croquet club, or it had come into existence almost by accident, one sunny summer, because a group of young people found themselves playing regularly together and getting a great deal of fun out of the game and each other's company. The organization was probably rather ramshackle, like the hutch that passed for a pavilion, but that was no great fault in a world that already was getting too full of organization. If funds did not permit the employment of a groundsman, a couple of volunteers would cut and roll the sward on Friday evening—and what more than that could you want ? The courts might be guilty of a bump here and there, or even of a gentle slope, but none of the players was so highly expert as to grow surly or grieve unduly over these little ups and downs. One and all played just for the fun of it, with no higher ambition than to win the American tournament on some holiday occasion, or to shine in the mixed doubles in partnership with the doctor's pretty daughter. The only cup they ever won was the cup of tea prepared by the ladies of the club—and how pleasant that was. How pleasant, in the middle of the set, to hear the chink-chink of the preparations, and how delightful, at the end of it, whether the match had been won or lost, to drop into a deckchair, and linger there over tea, and maybe strawberry tarts, and happy exchanges with the opposite sex. "A capital game," wrote the REV. FRANCIS KILVERT after his first essay in sphairistike, " but rather too hot for a summer's day." There were days when the members of the club felt just like that, and how long and cheerful it made the tea interval ! It was not Wimbledon, but it was very good.

STEALING THE FLOWER SHOW

IF there is one thing more delightful than looking at the flowers at a flower show it is looking at the people who are looking at the flowers. This is true both of our local show and of more serious events. At the first, to be sure, we meet " only " old friends and neighbours, but what could be pleasanter than that ? We have long ago ceased to complain of their conventionality or to wonder at their eccentricities ; we do not expect either to be vastly entertained or greatly shocked or unduly bored by anything they say or do ; but it is comforting to be surrounded by their familiar faces, just as it is reassuring to recognize on the trestle tables our old friends the vegetable marrows and the " vase of cut flowers (three varieties)." At the greater events—at the national rose show, for example, and on other occasions when the somewhat bleak shells of the Royal Horticultural Society's halls are transformed into new style Edens—it is different. The visitors have come, if not from the ends of the earth, then from all the soils of England, and they make a beautiful subject of study, though not in themselves quite so beautiful as the flowers are.

They have, to begin with, their accents. It would take HENRY HIGGINS, professor of phonetics, to do justice to these ; but anyone could guess that some at least of the speakers are professional gardeners from the country, and their wives, free for the day from the care of the kind of garden which owners throw open to the public in aid of the district nurses. They are not to be confused with those more prosperous professionals who own nurseries, and win medals for trade exhibits, and who are really successful business men in an extra-mural kind of way.

160

And no one could confuse either class with the amateurs—whether the men from the London suburbs in their business clothes, taking a quick look round in the lunch hour, or the smart young wives who have "taken up roses," or the quietly dressed ladies with rather old-fashioned hair styles, of ages between 50 and 70, who move purposefully from stand to stand, collecting catalogues and jotting down the names of new varieties in little note-books.

It is these last who "steal the show" for some observers. They cannot all be the vicar's wife, but they all look as though they might be. "*She's* been well fed," you hear them say approvingly as they stand before a bush of "Mrs. Sam McGredy." Or "Can you see the name of that one, dear? New S . . . or something. Surely not 'New Statesman.'" "No, dear, it's only 'new seedling.'" And so on. They have brought a leaf in an envelope, from a bush in their garden, to seek expert advice on how its ailment should be treated. And they stand entranced before each new beauty, with the rapt expression of music lovers at a concert. "Please do not smoke," say the notices—but even if they did not we should knock out our pipes for fear of doing harm to these rather faded roses.

M

THE GHOST GOES EAST

A T the risk of putting a new idea into the minds of the merry men of the Inland Revenue, it is irresistible to point out that they have forgotten ghosts. As between the owner of a stately home, complete with headless ancestor, working on night shifts, through the bedrooms, and one who cannot even boast of a miserable, vulgar little upstart of a poltergeist, they make no distinction. Ghosts are tax free. What is more, there are no restrictions on their export, although they might well be classified as irreplaceable, though invisible, assets. Board of Trade returns will be searched in vain for any mention, under any heading, of these national heirlooms. They are not to be found listed with spirits, alcoholic or industrial. So far as the state is concerned, they are trifles light as air, at liberty to go or stay as they please. And yet, so the Americans have just been ruefully reminding us, they earn dollars.

British ghosts, the complaint has arisen, are much more attractive than New Worldly ones. Britain is accused of competing unfairly in the tourist trade by conjuring up ghosts and haunted castles as attractions for visitors. " With this sort of competition," the lament concludes, " how can America keep her holiday makers at home ? " How indeed ? The precedent of M. RENÉ CLAIR's film apparition is discouraging to our rivals. It, if memory plays fair, was as fond of its ancient Scottish base as a cat is of a suburban house, known since kittenhood. But it did not take kindly to the transatlantic crossing. Ghosts are undeniably soft currency creatures. Who would be afraid of going up alone in an express elevator to the hundredth floor, even after being warned that the ghost

162

of a Wall Street speculator might appear half-way on the upward journey ?

Scepticism is the greatest occupational danger for ghosts and it would seem impossible to believe in them in a sky-scraper or, for the matter of that, in the replica of an Italian Renaissance palace built within easy commuting distance of Los Angeles. The only doubt that arises over the value of our competitive strength in this field—on this plane might be more apt—is provoked by uncertainty as to how far tourists swallow our time-honoured stories. Too often we have been our own ghosts' worst enemies. There was the conscientious one who accosted a guest wandering lost in a maze of dark corridors and exclaimed that it had been pacing them, nightly, for seven centuries. " Good " was the only reaction it got, " then you can tell me the way to the bathroom." Worse was the missionary who acknowledged cheerfully at breakfast that the family's ghost had paid him a bedside visit and who added, " Oh, no thanks, he did not keep me awake, he vanished as soon as I asked him for a subscription."

TAMING THE BENS

" *Wunderschön*," said a German writer contemplating Ben Lomond from a steamer on the loch. " But . . ." His " but " comprehended the reflections which MR. PETER BOYD, some twenty years later, has left with the delegates of the District Councils Association of Scotland. The German surmised there was a wonderful view from the summit of the Ben ; MR. BOYD knows there is—and from other Scottish mountains, too. The German was amazed that one had to walk to the top ; MR. BOYD is distressed that this should still be so. Both wanted the same thing. The German called it a *Schwebebahn;* MR. BOYD calls it an aerial railway. Aerial railways, he points out, would make the mountain tops of the Highlands accessible to tourists, who would then spend even more than the £50m. which the Scots are extracting from them every year.

If anyone has had MR. BOYD's idea before, it is hard to think why it has been neglected. It can hardly be a falling off of national enterprise. The Edinburgh Festival is a modern monument, in the nicest possible way, to the undimmed eye for the main chance. Of course, as a Lowland Scot would say, " there's aye a something." The peak attained, your non-walking mountaineer is not content to lie and watch the clouds. He wants to eat. He wants to drink. He wants to talk and make loud noises. He wants to write postcards. He wants, by some strange impulse, to buy souvenirs. He may want to stay the night. The summit is never the same once access is effortless. The Bens, or some of them, would be tamed. But if the Scots strain at this now, they convict themselves of illogicality. They have already made in the howes

164

the concessions that would be asked of them on the heights. Can they accept tourism as a national industry and differentiate between the top of Ben Nevis and the main street of Fort William ?

Undoubtedly the mountain railway would offer the chairborne tourist something he is not getting in the Highlands now. From the valleys, to which he is so largely bound, one can see the hills, but know almost nothing of them. An extraordinary amount of pleasure dwells in height. One part, the visual, anyone can enjoy. From the peaks of Arran one can look north to Glencoe and south-west to Ireland. From lesser hills above Mallaig, that ugly port at the end of the most beautiful railway in the world, there are Atlantic vistas hidden from the coast road. Every Ben has this kind of bounty. Nobody who climbs for pleasure will like the prospect of a torment of tourists on top of his favourite hill. But the Highlands are vast, and the tourist season is short. No matter what MR. BOYD stirs up, the walker in the hills will still have space for long days of unbroken solitude. When he has to meet the aerial excursionists he can wrap himself in 3,000ft. of moral superiority, and while moral superiority may be a vice, it is also a comfort.

WOMAN DRIVER

IF Chivalry ever passed his driving test, the lessons have long since been forgotten. On the road, sex warfare is total. Women and children first is all very well for sailors, those notoriously soft-hearted sentimentalists. The man at the wheel is made of sterner stuff. If two of him are alone in the same car, the odds are heavily in favour of them exclaiming to one another, at intervals only too regular and in tones of mingled irony and contempt, " Woman driver." What is said on the subject in clubs and in pubs, when no ladies are present, would not bear repeating in mixed company. It is most unfair—as can easily be shown from experience in peace and war. But, on the give-a-dog-a-bad-name principle, some people are eager to swallow any evidence against their sisters at the driving wheel. They will believe anything that they are told about the lack alike of road manners and of mechanical sense in the accused. Nor is such evidence lacking.

There is, for instance, the case of a motorist who was signalled to in a winding country lane by a lady solo in a limousine. When she had stopped him she asked, with a winning smile, if he would mind backing her car for her. She had overshot by some yards a gate through which she wished to proceed. The conscribed good Samaritan inquired whether there was anything wrong with her gears. " Oh, no," she said ; it was only that she had never been able to bring herself to master the trick of reversing. But she added, that was all right, as she had been driving far too long to have to face one of those tiresome tests.

More accomplished at the helm is the teen age girl whose gyrations in reverse were so prolonged and noisy that they lately attracted police attention. Her explanation went that she had been allowed to use the family car with a limit, which she had exceeded, on the mileage and she was just unwinding some of it. That is a cautionary tale for any father of spirit to tell his daughter at the learner stage. And, while he is about it, he might as well let his wife know that a lady has just been in trouble for deliberately backing her car into her husband's and has excused herself by pointing out that he had accidentally buckled her mudguard. But he had better keep these reports until his car is back safe in its garage ; otherwise, he may find himself stalling his engine or running out of petrol. The Nemesis that, as our mothers told us, would fix permanently the scowls on our faces when the wind changed, is, no doubt, ready to strike when we tell dreadful lies about our betters on the road.

TIME FOR BREAKFAST

THE reputation of the English breakfast—aromatic, substantial, gratifying to the inner man and socially satisfying—is familiar to all. The reality was sometimes rather different, and now it tends increasingly to depart from the tradition. The victuals, on the whole, are lighter than they were ; the emphasis is all on ease and speed in preparation and consumption ; and so in a great many homes the meal has been debaconized and cerealized. This simplified fare is swiftly disposed of in an atmosphere that is unlikely to be entirely care-free and relaxed. The curious convention, still not quite worn out, that father should be on time at the office, and the children at school, injects into the proceedings an element of unseemly haste. The kitchen may gleam with the latest equipment or the breakfast room delight the eye with three contrasting wallpapers, but the scene will refuse to resemble the happy tableaux in the porridge advertisements. The parties are uneasily aware that the winged chariots of the local transport system wait for no man, and the knowledge casts a shadow across the gay tablecloth—a shadow which such inconvenient events as school examinations and annual audits do nothing to chase away.

This morning, however—or on some other Saturday morning soon—all will be different. The family is going on holiday. This does not sensibly diminish the tension in the air, or reduce the call for speed in the disposal of the morning's refreshment. The tension, indeed, rises to new voltages ; the bustle makes the bustle of ordinary days appear by comparison a soothing calm. No one is relaxed—but everyone is happy. And to-morrow, and for an all-too-brief succession of days after that, they

168

will be relaxed as well. This is one of the many blessings of holiday—that breakfast may be savoured in peace. Not of course by the children—for whom peace at any time, and particularly at holiday time, would be synonymous with a living death—but by the adults of the party. They may and they will linger over breakfast like characters in a novel, talking of their letters and the news and the view and the weather and their plans for the day, with a rare feeling of being rich in hours. If they hurry at all it will be haste self-imposed, because something delightful is waiting to be done and not because there is a pile of housework round the corner or a train to town to be caught. It is all very good for the digestion, and it will not be surprising if the parties consume a large traditional breakfast—and feel all the better for it too.

ESCAPE ME EVER

"**B**ASINGSTOKE !" Sir Despard Murgatroyd was wont to cry in *Ruddigore* when poor mad Margaret seemed to be on the verge of one of her outbursts of passion ; to which she would demurely reply : " Basingstoke it is," and behave quite rationally. It was the wicked baronet's form of the " Now just relax, please " which is popularly understood to be the opening gambit in a psychiatrist's negotiations with a patient out of whom he is trying to prise deep secrets. Both demand an easing of tension, for the real benefits of relaxation lie in a contrast with the customary, a form of escapism more and more necessary in this age of speed and tension. So it is that a millionaire is the better able to enjoy the leisurely fruits of his riches from having started by selling newspapers in the streets ; that the business tycoon turns for mental solace from financial battles to literary battles of wits between detective and criminal. Contrast is here the key to escapism.

But the modern idea of escapist relaxation can be baffling. We read of a Paris fashion model who finds the pace of her calling too fast in that city. Instead of easing off in a cinema she flies over here as often as possible, because she finds Britain so relaxing. A bathchair at Bournemouth, perhaps, but has she ever tried to pour herself with the herd, during the rush hour, into the tube between Waterloo and the Bank ? Athletes, particularly, have odd notions on this subject. An Australian lawn tennis player was reported to have been able to relax when called upon to play only four doubles matches in a day instead of one singles. The caption beneath a picture of a man apparently doing a complicated Knees Up

Mother Brown announces that he is relaxing between heats of the hurdles, and MR. LEN HARVEY, discussing boxing tactics, says that he was lucky in that relaxation came naturally to him during long fights. Lucky indeed the man who could relax with fifteen stones of HERR NEUSEL in a small ring with him.

ELIZABETH BARRETT was on more familiar ground when she wrote : " When I have tired myself with writing, I am ready to be relaxed sufficiently with a little play with Flushie's pretty ears or a little dreaming off into a romance." It is true that visitors to her hermetically sealed room steered clear of her malodorous cur, and also that there was little physical contrast in her life, for until she married ROBERT BROWNING she rarely left her couch. But at least she went the whole hog in her escape from reality, and that is the essence of relaxation. As so often, the Chinese—it is to be hoped they are ready to acknowledge all the wisdom attributed to them—sum the matter up neatly in their proverb : " Of the thirty-six ways to escape the best is to run away."

APPEALING

THERE is a pleasant story, well authenticated, of one who went down to preach in chapel at his old school. It was a hot and somnolent day and the congregation were settling restfully down when he gave out his text " ' How's that ? ' said the bowler. ' Out,' said the umpire." The boys may have felt as did MR. PEPYS when he and some lady friends kept each other awake in church " from spite," but they sat up attentively throughout the sermon hoping for more. The sound of an appeal at cricket is a dreadfully expectant and intimidating one. The moment between that yell that goes up to heaven and the answer of the sphinx in the white coat is for those of us who watch, whether on the ground or in their own darkened rooms, almost unbearable. The appeal is made with such unhesitating and well simulated confidence that we can hardly believe it unjustified. That agreeable commentator, MR. FINGLETON, said the other day of his fellow country-men : " Australians generally do appeal confidently," and so they do. The umpire is a man of ice, not to be melted ; he knows their tricks and their manners ; but to us it seems that the finger of doom can scarcely stay down in face of so terrific a blare. The terror is the greater because so many people are caught at the wicket nowadays that we live in perpetual fear. " Good heavens," we exclaim in an agony of relief, " I was afraid he had touched it," as if to avoid touching the ball was the supreme object of the game. Moreover those who watch at home have seldom a clue ; neither their eyes nor their ears are good enough ; save for that demoniac shout the tragedy is a horribly silent one.

Just now and again we have an exquisite joy. It happened in TRUEMAN'S first over at Leeds during the third Test match. We could hear the click almost as if it had been the sound of a hammer. "How's that?" we screamed in unison and MCDONALD turned sadly but resignedly away. That was a rare treat, and to those whose cricket was of a village order or of a lower game at school it must sometimes occur that the one fate we did not fear was that of being caught at the wicket. If we missed the ball we missed it entirely ; if we did get a touch of it the catch was missed likewise, and if we had ever been given out we should have accused the umpire of cheating. These Langleys and Evanses make for us poor ignorant ones an unfamiliar game of it. Yet it gives us a certain delight, in the privacy of our own homes we can appeal recklessly and brutally. There can be no doubt that it is good savage fun. Anybody who has ever played in a fathers' match at a private school knows that in no circumstances can a gentleman appeal, and yet when a small leg is clearly in front of the wicket the shameful words have passed the barrier of his lips, not to be recalled and to meet with a cold, disapproving " Not out." It would have been so pleasant to get just one more wicket before he bowled on asphodel. " How's that ? " is surely a pardonable exuberance.

ASSIGNMENT TO CLEETHORPES

MOST of us have only an indistinct mental picture of what goes on in the Meteorological Office. No doubt there is a sort of operations room, in which minor bureaucrats equipped with billiard cues push symbols representing bright intervals and associated troughs of low pressure hither and thither across a huge map of the British Isles. Somewhere, presumably, there must be a weather-cock, the object of a tireless vigilance. The seismograph one visualizes as being kept in the basement ; it is possibly rather an old machine, but its brasswork and the plaque bearing the makers' name (Upshaft and Rigor, Shrewsbury, 1904) gleam like gold under the loving care of a retired coastguard. A small editorial department is responsible for the lapidary wording of the weather forecasts, or as they are now sometimes rather evasively called "synopses" ; here a rigid stylistic discipline reigns, and new recruits soon learn that attempts to strike a lyrical note by the use of such words as zephyr, balmy, torrid, and tempestuous are regarded with extreme disfavour. It may well have been in an endeavour to repress still further such deviationist tendencies that the Meteorological Office has adopted the practice of talking about " the general weather situation " when all it means (as far as ordinary mortals can see) is " the weather."

Life within this organization cannot be very exciting, and in hot weather there is keen competition among junior members of the staff for the duty of taking the No. 2 thermometer (which, unlike the ponderous No. 1, is portable) up to the Air Ministry roof and seeing what the temperature is. But in normal weather the general routine situation must be rather soul-destroying, and it is all the more refreshing to read of the special mission undertaken last week by the Meteorological Office's MR. L. H. STARR. MR. STARR, the report said, journeyed to Cleethorpes " to investigate complaints that the forecast for that part of the east coast had often been wrong." A lesser man would have travelled incognito, for not only had the forecast for the day on which he reached Cleethorpes been seriously misleading but MR. STARR was confronted on arrival by a MR. BOON, a night watchman at a pumping station who runs a rival meteorological service based—in the summer at any rate—on his observation of the antics of gnats and swallows.

Many an explorer, in the old days, saved himself from the tribal casserole by accurately predicting an eclipse of the sun, and it may be that MR. STARR has up his sleeve some similar *coup* with which to overawe the hostile natives of Cleethorpes. If he has not, his position is delicate and invidious. He is out on a limb. It is just possible that during his visit the weather at Cleethorpes will be accurately forecast from London ; but even if this happens it is virtually certain that it will not happen everywhere, and other aggrieved resorts will feel themselves entitled to the services of MR. STARR, either in the capacity of a whipping-boy or a medicine-man. He seems doomed to a career of peripatetic apology, to life on a razor's edge of uncertainty, to interminable disputations with gnat fanciers and the scrutineers of seaweed. Before the holiday season is over he may well be yearning for the familiar ruts of routine, for the Air Ministry roof and the cool, twilit basement in which the great brass-bound seismograph stolidly awaits its chance of making good.